£2.99 C14

CW00540533

When Was Jesus REALLY Born?

DAVID HAMSHIRE

PERISSOS MEDIA

Biblical Text: All Scripture quotations unless
otherwise indicated are taken from the New King
James Version®. Copyright © 1982 by Thomas
Nelson, Inc. Used by permission.
All rights reserved.

ISBN: 0992667712
ISBN-13: 978-0-9926677-1-9

Published by
PERISSOS MEDIA
An imprint of Perissos Group UK
PerissosMedia.com

For a FREE sample from this book,
please refer your family and friends to:

WhenWasJesusBorn.net/sample

DEDICATION

This book is dedicated to the
continuing remembrance of the birth
of *Yeshua HaMashiach*,
Jesus the Messiah.

"And the Word became flesh
and dwelt among us,
And we beheld His glory,
The glory as of the only begotten
of the Father,
Full of grace and truth."

John 1:14

"If I can only give my ideas
birth, shape and substance before I die,
they will work their own way to posterity."

William Alexander Madocks

1773 - 1828

ACKNOWLEDGMENTS

If I have understood correctly the numerous signs in Scripture for the day appointed for the birth of Jesus, then the accolade belongs to God; it is entirely His. If in this appraisal of *'When was Jesus REALLY born?'* I have made any errors, then the errors are entirely mine; nobody else is at fault.

One of the lessons which I have learnt about Scripture is not to ignore what at first may appear as seemingly minor detail, such as the swaddling cloths which Mary used to wrap Jesus in, or the manger in which she placed Him.

When the angel of the Lord appeared to Bethlehem's shepherds to announce the birth of Jesus, included in the acknowledgement was not only where the shepherds would find God's Son, but also detail of a sign to indicate that this new-born child was destined to become their Saviour and Israel's promised Messiah.

The sign, given in advance of Jesus' birth, is in the meaning of the swaddling cloths and the manger. Seen in tandem – and with the benefit of hindsight – the two references are a most remarkable sign that only God could have known about.

Signs in the Bible are provided to help the unknowing to understand God. The fact that God has provided so many tell-tale signs concerning the timing for His Son's birth, is perhaps the greatest wonder of the Bible. For those who believe in God, it should come as no surprise that we can read about the timing of Jesus' birth recorded in Scripture long before Jesus was born.

My prayer in presenting these five signs – *'When was Jesus REALLY born?'* – is that when you have finished reading about the miraculous timing for Jesus' birth, that your own acknowledgement, like that of the *"...multitude of the heavenly host"* who praised God for Jesus' birth, will also be: *"Glory to God in the highest, and on earth peace, goodwill toward men!"* (Luke 2:14). This was the acknowledgement of the multitude of the heavenly host; may it always be our acknowledgment.

David Hamshire

CONTENTS

DAVID HAMSHIRE

FOREWORD

I have known David Hamshire for nearly fifty years. David and I first met while serving in the Royal Air Force at RAF Abingdon. I was then, and remain, struck by his love of the Lord and his warm and infectious personality. At my wedding in 1966, when I had to choose someone to be my 'Best Man', there was no question in my mind as to who it should be. David was my first and only choice.

One of David's great attributes is his courage. In his first book, *'He must increase…'*, David tells of an occasion when he discovered a stately home on fire and with very little thought of the danger involved, he helped rescue many valuable paintings and works of art.

In this book, David has again demonstrated his courage. I know of no comparable thesis on the very emotive subject of Christmas and the date of Jesus' birth. David readily admits that he could be wrong, but I suspect that he could be right!

Some years ago, I did a series of programmes on Revelation TV entitled, "Sorry, I don't celebrate Christmas – I'm a Christian!" The programs were hugely popular, and I received very many letters and emails from Christians who were fed-up with the secularization and commercialization of this festival. Recently, I received a quotation from a seven-year-old boy who said, *"God, did you think that Christmas would end up like this when you started it?"*

My programs and the subsequent talks that I gave were all negative – they demonstrated without any doubt that we are wrong to think that Jesus was born on December 25th. The talks also encouraged many who for years had grave concerns, but had never had the courage to voice them. On the other hand, a number folk took exception and demonstrated that they had a strong emotional attachment to this season. Many said that it was a wonderful opportunity to share the Gospel, but my friend David Pawson did some research and discovered that fewer people became Christians at Christmastime than at any other time of the year!

In this fascinating book, David Hamshire has taken the gallant but unusual step of coming to the subject of Jesus' birth in a new, refreshing and positive way. Please read this book with an open mind. You may well discover new and exciting truths about our wonderful Saviour and Lord.

David Winter
July 2013

INTRODUCTION

The title I chose for this book concerns *Yeshua HaMashiach* – Jesus the Messiah – and when He was born. For centuries, possibly for nearly two thousand years, the question as to when Jesus was born has been hotly debated. Many theories as to when Mary gave birth to her firstborn Son have been discussed but there exists, as far as I'm aware, no universal acceptance.

Indeed, for the majority of those who believe in Jesus, their opinion is likely to be divided, so that if there is no agreement as to when Jesus was born, then it is quite acceptable for believers to remember His birth at Christmas. But, like many, I do not believe that Jesus was born at Christmas. I do, however, have a suggestion as to when He was born, although to nominate an actual day/date for Jesus' birth has not been straightforward; I have no academic or theological credentials.

The first four of five signs for the timing of Jesus' birth became apparent over a relatively brief period of time, but I then delayed in considering publication because I was not sure if I should do so. However, more recently, because I believe the Bible is absolutely clear about when Jesus was born, and that it may be helpful for others to consider what is the most appropriate day/date for His birth, then perhaps now is the right time to explain why God's chosen date is so important and so pertinent.

The implication for stating an actual day/date for when Jesus was born may be queried, especially by those who may have spent years in studying the Bible. Are readers likely to take my suggestion seriously, or will I be ridiculed? If I am ridiculed, does it matter? It was then that I was challenged by this saying: *"If you are alive you can change things. If you are dead you can't."* A very simple truth, so what should I do?

In helping me to decide, a reminder of the wisdom of Hillel the Elder was the final prompt: *"If not me, who? If not now, when?"* Profound wisdom, yet simple enough in persuading me that now was the right time to make known the detail of what, I believe, God has shown me.

For Gentiles who believe in Jesus the Christ, and for Jewish people who believe in Yeshua HaMashiach (Jesus the Messiah), the fact that in the pages that follow I have provided five pieces of evidence for the day/date when Jesus was born will, I hope, be of some interest. If the date I am suggesting is plausible, then there exists an alternative day (and an alternative lifestyle?) for those who wish to remember Jesus' birth.

It would be very unlikely for only one reader to ask the following question: "Although Christmas Day may not be the correct date, does it matter if this is the time when we remember Jesus' birth?" In responding to such a question, I would say: "Many years ago I had the privilege of meeting Queen

Elizabeth II, and for just a few minutes the two of us chatted happily together. If for some reason I had decided not to respect her as Queen of the United Kingdom and the Commonwealth, but saw her as just another citizen of the United Kingdom, then no matter how polite I may have been, I would have been wrong in not showing her the respect she deserves.

Respect for God and respect for His decision as to when He would send His Son is why it is important to seek the truth and not be misled. Please note: The birth of Jesus is historical, not futuristic, as with His second coming. I'm not suggesting a date for Jesus' return, only a date for when He was born in Bethlehem and why God chose this particular date from all other dates available to Him.

The Bible, of course, must hold the secret as to when Jesus was born and it is from the pages of Scripture on which I have based my discovery. In John's gospel there exists a number of intriguing events, each spoken of as *Signs*. In chapter four, for example, we read of a nobleman who asked Jesus to come and heal his son. Jesus does not go to the nobleman's house but says to the man: "Go your way; your son lives" (verse 51). We are then told by John that this was the second *Sign* that Jesus performed (verse 54). What was the *Sign*? Was it the fact that the man's son was healed, or was it that he was healed at the "...seventh hour" (verse 52)? When no one who observed this miracle had either a watch or a clock to note the time of the boy's

13

healing, does it not seem strange that the time of the miracle was recorded and then later included in John's account of the life of Jesus? Therefore, in the very detailed historical record about Jesus, what is so important about time?

In the next chapter of John, Jesus said: *"You search the Scriptures, for in them you think you have eternal life; and these are they which testify of Me"* (John 5:39). The Scriptures that Jesus was referring to are not the New Testament Scriptures but the Scriptures of the Hebrew Bible, known to Jewish people as the *Tanakh*, and to Gentile believers as the Old Testament. It is in these Scriptures that the evidence as to when Jesus was born (and when He was to die) can be found.

About two thousand years ago when Jesus was sitting with His disciples on the Mount of Olives and looking across the Kidron Valley towards Jerusalem, He informed His disciples that the date of His second coming was known only by the Father (Matthew 24:36). If the Father knew then when Jesus would return, would the Father not have known beforehand the date for when Jesus would be born? If correct, what are the *Signs* in Scripture that we should be relying on, rather than continuing to observe a date for Jesus' birth that is widely known to be wrong?

Today we live in an era that has become known as the age of 'Information Technology', where the majority, including those living in the earth's most remotest regions, have access to a World-Wide-Web of information. For God's people, the most reliable resource for information about Jesus will always be the Bible, and this book explains the importance and the relevance of the date chosen for Jesus' birth. Searches on the Internet are unlikely to reveal what is available in the Bible, but it is from God's Word that I have come to appreciate *Five Signs* for the date when Jesus was born. Of course, any one *Sign* is significant, but it is within the *Fifth Sign* that the metaphorical significance of Jesus' birth was first revealed, perhaps thousands of years before His birth.

In February 2013 I visited Israel to spend a few days with some friends in Tel Aviv. Before my visit I had planned to spend one day in Jerusalem. Jerusalem I love, especially the Old City, so when visiting Jerusalem I always try and walk the streets of the Old City and visit the Garden of Gethsemane, the garden where Jesus prayed to His Father and was arrested. In the Garden of Eden, the battle against temptation was lost, but in the Garden of Gethsemane, the battle against sin was decided.

During my one day visit to Jerusalem, I met a Gentile believer and discussed my belief that in the year of His birth Jesus was born on the Jewish Day of Atonement. Unfortunately, I used terms such as *"If Jesus was born on the Day of Atonement..."* or *"maybe..."* or similar expressions of uncertainty, which must have given the impression that I was confused. I was rebuked – and in the strongest

15

manner possible! *"If you believe Jesus was born on the Day of Atonement, you should not be using such words as 'if' and 'maybe.' If you believe the Day of Atonement was the day when Jesus was born, then say so, and without your doubts!"* Somewhat offended, I left him, but later came to value his advice. I knew I had shown uncertainty about my conviction, but never again. In the future I would state what I believe because my belief is based on God's ability to make decisions and to implement those decisions in order to achieve His purposes.

In continuing to consider the date chosen for Jesus' birth, I can think of no alternative day or reason for selecting another day. Five scriptural reasons for the selection of the Day of Atonement have been sufficient to convince me that there is no alternative day. If there is only one day in the annual cycle of the cosmos that is appropriate for Jesus' birth, why look for another?

In explaining the *Five Signs* for Jesus' birth, my prayer is that if you have not seen these *Signs* before, then by considering them now, you will understand why the Day of Atonement is a very important day. It was the Father of Jesus who set this day aside; it was He who made this day *Holy*. For Jewish people, it remains a most *Awesome Day*.

David Hamshire

WHAT AN AWESOME DAY

"And it came to pass in those days that a decree went out from Caesar Augustus that all the world should be registered. This census first took place while Quirinius was governing Syria. So all went to be registered, everyone to his own city. Joseph also went up from Galilee, out of the city of Nazareth, into Judea, to the city of David, which is called Bethlehem, because he was of the house and lineage of David, to be registered with Mary, his betrothed wife, who was with child. So it was, that while they were there, the days were completed for her to be delivered. And she brought forth her firstborn Son, and wrapped Him in swaddling cloths and laid Him in a manger, because there was no room for them in the inn" (Luke 2:1–7).

~ ~ ~

On Friday, July 1, 2011, Jonathan Sacks, the Chief Rabbi of Great Britain, was the guest speaker on BBC Radio Four's *'Thought for the Day'* program. In sharing his thought, the Rabbi said: *"...in one sense life is a lottery, because none of us chooses when and where to be born."* For you and for me, for everyone, how true; not one of us had any say in the matter. But there has been one exception, and his name is Jesus. Among those who have experienced a physical birth, only Jesus knew in advance when and where He would be born. If you consider this assumption to be absurd, remember that Jesus once said to His disciples only a few hours before He was led away to be crucified, that He had been able to share in the glory of His Father "...before the world was" (John 17:5).

By faith I believe that Jesus existed before He experienced a physical birth; therefore, His miraculous conception in the womb of Mary is an event I have accepted. The choice of Mary to be Jesus' mother and for Him to enter her body and grow to maturity, was indeed remarkable and I do understand why some people find it hard to accept. However, the conception of Jesus, followed by His birth, death and resurrection, were included in God's plan for His Son. For those who believe in Jesus, their faith is based on Jesus as being God's Son and that God has the authority and the ability to implement His plans at the time and place of His choosing.

For the place of Jesus' birth, Micah prophesied that it would take place in Bethlehem, and the writer of Psalm 2 recorded when He was to be born: "You are My Son, today I have begotten You." Or, as this verse is rendered in The Complete Jewish Bible, "You are My Son, today I became Your father" (Psalm 2:7). When reading this verse, I noted that a certain day for Jesus' birth does appear to have been chosen. Therefore, the question for those who believe in Jesus is this: Which day is the psalmist referring to?

Before I explain how I came to see *Five Signs* for when Jesus was most likely to have been born (and with regard to the actual day/date, I am now totally convinced), I would like to recall two biblical disciplines that are basic to Jesus' birth and that are frequently referred to in the Bible.

Appointed Times and Appointed Places

For most Jewish people and also many Christians, they regularly observe what are referred to in Scripture as the *'Seven Feasts of the Lord'*. Described in Leviticus chapter twenty-three, the Feasts are times of remembrance when Jewish people recall certain historical events, such as Passover (their Exodus from slavery in Egypt), as well as current happenings, such as their annual harvest times. The dates associated with these festivals were originally determined not by Jewish people, but by God, and it is quite correct to refer to these Feasts as being the Lord's *Appointed Times*.

Appointed Times is the first of the two disciplines we need to understand and a close examination of the Feasts of the Lord (and also the Sabbath) explains God's involvement in allocating both *Time* and *Times* to His instructions.

We will return to this discipline later, but what is important for us to understand is that for God *Time*, *Times* and *Timing* are hugely important because God frequently incorporates time in the working out of His divine timetable.

The second discipline refers to God's *Appointed Places* and there are numerous references in

Scripture that indicate God's choice of a particular location for where an event, or events, will one day take place. For example, in Exodus chapter twenty, after God gave to the Children of Israel the Ten Commandments, we read in verse twenty-four: "An altar of earth you shall make for Me, and you shall sacrifice on it your burnt offerings and your peace offerings, your sheep and your oxen. <u>In every place where I record My name</u> I will come to you, and I will bless you." (Author's underlining)

One particular place where God was to record His name was, of course, Jerusalem. "Since the day that I brought My people out of the land of Egypt, I have chosen no city from any tribe of Israel in which to build a house that My name might be there, nor did I chose any man to be a ruler over My people Israel. Yet I have chosen Jerusalem, that My name may be there, and I have chosen David to be over My people Israel" (2 Chronicles 6:5–6).

Here we see that God not only foreordained David to be a ruler over His people, but that He also chose Jerusalem as a place where He would record His name. David's son Solomon spoke of this when he dedicated the first temple.

And Solomon prayed, "Yet regard the prayer of Your servant and his supplication, O Lord my God, and listen to the cry and the prayer which Your servant is praying before You, that Your eyes may be open toward this temple day and night, <u>toward the place where You said You would put Your</u>

name, that You may hear the prayer Your servant makes toward this place" (2 Chronicles 6:19-20). (Author's underlining)

Ezekiel also recorded God's *Appointed Place* as being Jerusalem when he wrote "THE LORD IS THERE" (Ezekiel 48:35). Jerusalem was and continues to be, God's *Appointed Place*, for it is where Jesus died to become God's appointed sacrifice for sin and where, after three days, Jesus would rise from death.

Bethlehem was also an *Appointed Place* and the prophet Micah was inspired to prophecy and record, "But you, Bethlehem Ephrathah, though you are little among the thousands of Judah, yet out of you shall come forth to Me the One to be Ruler in Israel, whose goings forth are from of old, from everlasting" (Micah 5:2). The little hamlet of Bethlehem (meaning, *'The House of Bread'*) was God's choice for the location for His Son's birth.

Therefore, concerning Jesus, there are two *Appointed Places*: Bethlehem, where He was to be born; and Jerusalem, where He was to die, each decided upon many years before His birth.

If *Appointed Times* and *Appointed Places* are two of God's disciplines, then it must follow that not only *when* and *where* Jesus died is important, but *when* and *where* He was born must also be important. One of my objectives in this study has been to consider these two disciplines, *Time* and *Place*, but particularly *Time*. If we are to believe that Jesus is

God's Son and that we can only know God through Him, is it unreasonable to suggest that the day when He was born (when Mary laid Him in a manger), that that day was and continues to be a very important day? If true, then the date for Jesus' birth must be hugely significant.

In seeking the Lord about this, I believe He has now given me *Five Signs* that indicate when the birth of Jesus took place, and by this I mean on which day Jesus was born. In the year Jesus was born, I believe His birth took place on the tenth day of the Hebrew month Tishrei, the Jewish Day of Atonement. In believing this I have summarized the *Five Signs* as follows.

1. The First Sign: The birth of Jesus as related to *'Time'*. That which God sanctified; He made Holy.

2. The Second Sign: The birth of Jesus as observed in *'The Seven Feasts of the Lord'*. God's call to remembrance.

3. The Third Sign: The birth of Jesus as observed in the unfolding of God's Word and His servant Elijah – John the Baptist.

4. The Fourth Sign: The birth of Jesus as God's High Priest. Jesus having been chosen from *"...the foundation of the world."*

5. The Fifth Sign: The birth of Jesus as seen by what is good. *'Truth unchanged from the dawn of time.'*

THE FIRST SIGN

The birth of Jesus as related to *'Time'*.

That which God sanctified; He made Holy.

It was over a period of about two years that I considered the date for Jesus' birth and if the date was recorded in the Bible or in ancient history. If the Bible is *His-Story*, then perhaps the date of Jesus' birth was recorded in the Bible; it's just that within the Church generally there appears to be no agreed consensus about when His birth took place. The fact that the majority of Christians celebrate Jesus' birth at Christmas (yet many are aware that He was not born at Christmas) seems to suggest that because the time of His birth is reckoned as being unknown, that it is entirely acceptable to remember His birth as having taken place on December 25. In a similar way, although Jesus was crucified on the eve of Passover, most Christians remember His death at the time of Easter.

Lunar and Solar activity – the controllers of time

What I first began to observe is the link between the lunar calendar which Jewish people observe, with the solar calendar which Gentiles follow. In understanding these two patterns of time, what is clear is that Jesus observed the lunar (Hebrew) calendar, but His life (His years) was in accordance with the solar calendar. The fact that the timing for His birth and His death can be traced to both calendars is quite remarkable, yet it is also logical.

Therefore, my starting point in seeking to understand when Jesus was born was to learn about lunar and solar activity and to discover how the two are related; for indeed a link must exist if we are to believe that Jesus is the Son of God and that He was involved with His Father in creation. The birth of Jesus could not have been a random event in that the timing of His birth was of no consequence. The day when Jesus was born was the day when God became: *"Emanuel, God with us."* Surely, it must have been an important day? If, as Jonathan Sacks suggests: *"Science is the search for explanation, and Religion is the search for meaning"*, then any search of the universe and the Bible in tandem should provide both the *explanation* and the *meaning* for when Jesus was born.

I am aware that I cannot prove when Jesus was born, as I cannot prove that Moses ever existed, so maybe not all will agree with my reasoning? However, since I published (March 2011) my first book which detailed the first of two signs for when, I believe, Jesus was born, many have told me that they agree with my thesis.

One scholar who understands Greek, Hebrew, and Latin (which, I must confess I do not understand), has said he entirely agrees with my reasoning for when Jesus was most likely to have been born.

WHEN WAS JESUS REALLY BORN?

Those who believe God created the world believe also that the world is maintained by God. Marcus du Sautoy, a professor of mathematics, has said: "My big thesis is that although the world looks messy and chaotic, if you translate it into the world of numbers and shapes, patterns emerge and you start to understand why things are the way they are. It's numbers that dictate how the world must be."

That a leading professor has recognized that there are patterns in creation which include mathematical formulae and design, should not surprise us. God's *'Textbook for Life'* (the Bible) explains via Hebrew thought regarding numbers that it is from here we should commence if we want to understand God's ways. For example, the number *Seven* frequently appears in Scripture as a sign of *Being Full*, or *Satisfied With*, and is an indication of God's association with what is often regarded as *'Spiritual Perfection'.* The following are a few well-known examples:

- The *Seven Days* of the week; the *Seventh* the *Sabbath*.
- The *Seven Feasts of the Lord*; God's appointed festivals.
- The *Seven Stars of Pleiades* – Job 38:31.
- The *Seven Sign Miracles* of Jesus in John's gospel.
- The *Seven Words of Jesus* from the cross.
- God's messages to the *Seven Churches* (Revelation 1–3).

25

- Heaven's Scroll which has *Seven Seals*, to be opened only by Jesus (Revelation 5–8).

An appreciation of the sign of *Seven* in the Bible is the first step in observing design and how to begin to understand the Bible.

Ten is also an important number and ten often appears in Scripture to reveal aspects of *'The Perfection of Divine Order'*. E. W. Bullinger, in his book *'Number in Scripture'*, comments as follows on the importance of ten: *"It implies nothing is wanting; that the number and order are perfect; that the whole cycle is complete."* For example: The Ten Commandments.

Very many years ago the numbers *Seven* and *Ten* became linked to the most significant day in Jewish history. Yom Kippur, the Day of Atonement, is observed by Jewish people as the most important of the Seven Festivals which they keep annually.

Atonement means: *'To cover the sins of God's people with the blood of the sacrifice'* and the work of atonement enables the penitent to start afresh. Yom Kippur is a day of new life, of new beginnings; and God told Moses to set this day aside on: "…the tenth day of this seventh month shall be the Day of Atonement" (Leviticus 23:27).

Why did God say to Moses that the Children of Israel were to keep the "tenth day of this seventh month" holy? What is it about the Day of

Atonement that makes this particular day so special that for Jewish people it is still a holy day?

Christmas Day is the time when most people recall the birth of Jesus, but for the majority of them they are probably unaware that Christmas originates from a pagan festival from Babylon. In the fourth century A.D., Pope Julius I adopted a Babylonian festival as the time when members of the Roman Catholic Church should remember the birth of Jesus.

For Jewish people, Babylon was where their ancestors experienced exile, persecution and death, and so for Jewish people Babylon was the worst possible location from where to select a pagan festival to celebrate the birth of the Jewish Messiah. To have introduced a non-Jewish festival as the day when Jesus was born has been most effective in moving the Church away from its Hebrew origins.

The New Testament states that believers should remember the death of Jesus, and this they do at *'The Lord's Supper'*, but is the Bible silent when it comes to remembering His date of birth? If believers are to remember Jesus' birth, then it follows that when He was born must be important. Surely, an incorrect date is unhelpful and lacks any real meaning. As we consider our own lives, is it not true that a person's date of birth is usually of greater importance than their place of birth? Our place of birth may be of some significance, but our date of birth is a reference about us and when we became a living person. It was Micah who prophesied where Jesus would be born; His birthplace was to be in Bethlehem. But did nobody prophesy when Jesus would be born, or record the date when He was born?

When Jesus died, the time was accurately recorded; it was at the ninth hour on the 14th day of the month Nisan, the eve of Passover. This detail can be helpful when determining when Jesus was born, for Luke wrote that when he began His public ministry, Jesus was "…about thirty years of age" (Luke 3:23). Thirty was the age when Joseph (in whose life there are many similarities to Jesus) began his life's calling (Genesis 41:46). Age thirty was also the time when those who served in the Tabernacle commenced their priestly ministry (Numbers 4:3). There should be no difficulty in understanding that Jesus was thirty years of age when he commenced what the Father had planned for Him to do.

Weeks and Years

In Hebrew thought, a week can be used to describe a period of days, weeks, or years; and the prophet Daniel wrote that "…Messiah shall be cut off, but not for Himself" and that this would take place "…in the middle of the week," to "…bring an end to sacrifice and offering" (Daniel 9:26–27). As agreed by many Bible commentators, we can conclude from Daniel's prophecy that the ministry of Jesus was designed to last for three and a half years before He would be *Cut Off* and die, the same expression as used by Isaiah: "For He was cut off from the land of the living" (Isaiah 53:8). Therefore, when Jesus died, He would have been thirty three and a half years of age.

Hebrew years are based on the moon's circumnavigation of the earth and are known as lunar years. But lunar years always lag behind solar years because solar years are measured by the earth's travel around the sun; therefore solar years are longer, by about eleven days. About every three years extra days in the form of an extra month are added to the Hebrew lunar calendar to bring its cycle into line with the solar cycle. This is carried out so that lunar years do not get out of phase with the earth's seasons. For example, in the year 2011 an additional month was added to the Hebrew calendar to make 2011 a lunar leap year.

It was in 2010 that I began to consider lunar and solar cycles and to carry out a basic calculation. By referring to 2009 and 2010 lunar cycles, I then superimposed their detail over a solar cycle for each of the two years and then worked backwards from the 14th day of Nisan in 2010 (Monday, March 29th), the day in the lunar calendar when Jesus died, half a solar year.

The task was quite simple, but it was the outcome that greatly surprised me. It took me precisely to the Day of Atonement in the previous year, the tenth day of Tishrei (Monday, September 28th, 2009).

Previously, I was unaware that there could be a lunar and solar connection between the Day of Atonement and the day appointed for the preparation for Passover, the day when Jesus died; however, the two dates, exactly half a solar year apart (180 degrees of a solar cycle), appear to make perfect sense as an indicator for the time when Jesus was born. At His birth, Jesus' destiny was that He would become the fulfilment of what God had said should take place on the Day of Atonement. At His death, He would fulfil and become God's Passover sacrifice (1 Corinthians 5:7).

The two dates for the Day of Atonement and for Passover were not selected at random; they were chosen by God who then informed Moses of His decision. Abraham Joshua Heschel (1907-1972), in his book, 'The Sabbath', provides the most likely reason for this: *"God is not in things of space, but in moments of time. Yet the likeness of God can be found in time, which is eternity in disguise."* Heschel also states, *"The bible is more concerned with time than with space. It (the Bible) sees the world in the dimension of time."* The Bible is very clear: Time is Holy. "Then God blessed the seventh day and sanctified it (made it Holy)" (Genesis 2:3).

On a number of occasions Jesus said that *His Hour* (*His Time*) had not yet come, such as when He turned water into wine, or when some tried to kill Him prematurely. Only when His *Hour* was completed did God permit Jesus to die in order for His birth and His death (and His years in between) to become the fulfilment for the Day of Atonement and the Passover observances.

The synoptic Gospels (Matthew, Mark and Luke) each state that Jesus died at the *Ninth Hour* (three o'clock in the afternoon) on the 14th day of Nisan. If the birth of Jesus occurred at precisely one hundred and eighty degrees into the solar cycle from when He died – which is half a solar year, or one hundred and eighty-two days, fourteen hours, fifty-four minutes and thirty seconds as calculated in reverse from the time of His death – then the birth of Jesus could have occurred at five and a half minutes after midnight on the Day of Atonement, thirty-three and a half solar years earlier.

I'm not stating that this is the precise time when Jesus was born, although it could so easily have been so. I simply want to point out that by referring to lunar and solar activity that a simple calculation is possible to show that it can be exactly half a solar year from the Day of Atonement in one year, to the day of preparation for Passover in the following year.

Is it possible that God did indeed plan for the birth of Jesus to be linked to the sequential timing of the world, the sun and the moon which He had created?

The heavens are indeed God's perfect clock. "The heavens declare the glory of God; and the firmament shows His handiwork" (Psalm 19:1). And in Hebrews we read: "God …has in these last

31

days spoken to us by His Son …through whom also He made the worlds" (Hebrews 1:1 & 2).

These words from the book of Hebrews appear to suggest that the writer was inspired to record a clear link between the life and ministry of Jesus, and the establishment of the universe. In Genesis we read that when God created the lights in the "…firmament of the heavens," they were to be for "signs and seasons, and for days and years" (Genesis 1:14).

I'm sure everyone understands the nature of the *Seasons*, *Days* and *Years*, but are the *lights* which God created sometimes used as *Signs*? For the wise men who came to Jerusalem to see the One who had been born "King of the Jews", they came to worship Him because they had seen "…His star" (a *Sign?*) and they wanted to pay Him homage and to present to Him their gifts (Matthew 2:1–2).

At His first coming, Jesus fulfilled many of the Hebrew Bible's prophetic *Signs*. At His second coming, He will fulfil further prophetic *Signs* and also heavenly *Signs*, some of which He described to His disciples and which will include, "…signs in the sun, in the moon, and in the stars; and on the earth distress of nations, with perplexity, the sea and the waves roaring; men's hearts failing them from fear and the expectation of those things which are coming on the earth, for the powers of the heavens will be shaken" (Luke 21:25–26).

Two New Years

Confusing to some possibly, but Hebrew years feature two New Years. The Hebrew Civil Calendar begins in the autumn, with the month Tishrei. If Jesus was born on the tenth day of Tishrei, the Day of Atonement, it was appropriate, for His birth was a civil event. The Hebrew Religious Calendar begins in the spring, with the month Nisan. Jesus died on the 14th day of Nisan, the eve of Passover, for His death was a religious event.

There is a popular hymn which begins with these words. "Jesus is Lord creation's voice proclaims it, for by His power each tree and flower was planned and made. Jesus is Lord the universe declares it, Sun, Moon and Stars in Heaven cry Jesus is Lord." But do the *Sun*, the *Moon* and the *Stars* each declare that *JESUS IS LORD*? For that is what we sing.

Another hymn of praise and thanksgiving that is greatly loved by many is "Great is Thy faithfulness, O God my Father." The second verse includes these words: "Sun, Moon and Stars in their courses above, join with all nature in manifold witness, to Thy great faithfulness, mercy and love."

Finally, the hymn "Praise my soul, the King of Heaven; to His feet thy tribute bring...." In verse five we sing: "Angels help us to adore Him, Ye behold Him face to face: Sun and Moon, bow down before Him; dwellers all in time and space."

It appears that some of our greatest hymn writers have observed clear links to that which God has created, including the sun and the moon which control *Time*, and His Son, the Lord Jesus.

This is not to say that we should regard the sun and the moon in some kind of solar worship activity such as practiced by the idolatrous priests in the days leading up to Josiah's reign, when they "…burned incense to Baal, to the sun, to the moon, to the constellations and to all the host of Heaven" (2 Kings 22:5). Nevertheless, the two *lights* that were made to control the *Seasons*, the *Days* and the *Years*, God also designed them to act as *Signs* (Genesis 1:14) so that we might observe and understand something of the nature and wonder of God and which includes God's promise of the birth and death of His Son, Jesus.

During my school years I was not taught the basics of the solar system. Also, during the thousands of church meetings I've attended, speakers seem to avoid discussing creation's secrets which have resulted in the seasons, days and years. It is only as a result of personal study and curiosity that I can now begin to appreciate the dynamics of creation upon which we are all so dependent. My study has also helped me to observe how Jesus' birth was linked to creation (see *Sign Five*), which has resulted in my observation becoming a journey of new and immense discovery. After so many years of ignorance, at last a veil has been removed from my understanding of the universe and Jesus' birth.

For many years I've known that a calendar year lasts for three hundred and sixty-five days and that during every fourth year an extra day is added to keep our years in step with the earth's orbit around the sun. To satisfy my curiosity as to the actual time it takes for us to travel millions of miles through space, I turned to the Internet. The time taken for the earth to circumnavigate the sun is three hundred and sixty-five days, five hours and forty-nine minutes. It was this period of time that I divided by two which led me to discover that it is exactly half a solar year from the Day of Atonement in one year, to the eve of Passover in the following year.

What is also riveting is that we are all travelling through space at a speed of approximately 66,600 miles per hour and that each year in our journey around the sun we will have travelled 584 million miles. And, in our travel through both time and space, it is to a pre-programmed accuracy of less than one second a year. Included in this blend of time and travel is the moon, which orbits the earth once every twenty-nine and a half days. The moon's orbit of the earth explains why Hebrew lunar years are shorter than solar years.

The earth is also tilted from the perpendicular and it is this angle that is responsible for the Earth's seasons, which in turn affects our weather and life's ability to survive, mainly through the seasonal harvests. The earth's tilt from the vertical by twenty-three degrees (according to technologists the most appropriate angle) is a number that we will return to in *Sign Two*.

The earth, with its cyclical link with the sun and the moon, embraces the very secrets of creation. Creation confirms design and the three – the earth, the sun and the moon – are a prime example of a perfect tripartite relationship, because God made the three to function as one. To see that Jesus is the One "...through whom also He made the worlds" (Hebrews 1:2) is to see that God works to a plan and that this includes the relationship He has with His Son, the Holy Spirit, and with His people.

That the birth–day of Jesus could be associated with the creation of the solar system and the cycle of the *Seven Feasts of the Lord* as prescribed by God to Moses, which includes the Day of Atonement, should be sufficient to convince everyone that the birth of Jesus is not so incomprehensible as some may have imagined, but that His birth-day can be seen as a help to faith and as a *Sign* that God wants to relate to us, so long as we are willing to respect, trust, and obey God.

In choosing the date for the Day of Atonement, I've stated that it could not have been a random selection of just any date. God must have had a reason for selecting this date. The Day of Atonement should be seen as a *Sign* of God's relationship through His Son with His people and is explained in the atonement remembrance that continues to be observed by Jewish people to this day.

In the film adaption of Hugh Lofting's novel *Doctor Dolittle*, Doctor Dolittle's (Rex Harrison) co-star Emma Fairfax (Samantha Eggar) with her eyes closed, sticks a pin in a map to help the enigmatic doctor to locate the site where he believes he will find the elusive Sea Snail. Emma places the pin on Sea Star Island, a floating island in the middle of the Atlantic Ocean. Boarding their frail vessel, the intrepid crew set sail to find the island and the Sea Snail. The story is charming and witty, but only imaginary, as fiction usually is.

Are we to assume that God placed a pin into the module of time and space and decided that this was when and where He would send His Son? Of course not. God's involvement in carrying out His purposes was not determined by chance, by a pin, but was in accordance to His preordained will. The date God chose for the Day of Atonement is just one detail of His eternal grace and favor plan.

A few years ago I invested in a satellite navigation device (*Sat Nav*), which utilizes earth observation technology to make it function. In planning my journeys, I am now able to:

- Program from where I want to start my journey.
- Input where my journey will end.
- Note the time it will take for me to complete my journey.
- Show me my speed throughout the journey.

- Be advised of any speed restrictions.
- Listen to instructions, for example to turn left or right.
- Observe the network of roads along the route.

Is God inferior to a *Sat Nav*? Of course not! Since time began God has guided His people to understand His truth and His ways and Scripture confirms that included in His knowledge was when and where Jesus (the *Light of the World*) would be *cut off*, He would die. Therefore, God must also have known when and where His Son was to be born. The words from Isaac Watts famous hymn "Give to Our God Immortal Praise", epitomizes it so clearly:

He built the earth, He spread the sky,
And fixed the starry lights on high;
Wonders of grace to God belong,
Repeat His mercies in your song.

He fills the sun with morning light,
He bids the moon direct the night;
His mercies ever shall endure,
When suns and moons shall shine no more."

The psalmist in observing, "The Heavens declare the Glory of God; and the firmament shows His handiwork" (Psalm 19:1) has been followed by a number of hymn writers (four of whom I have already quoted) who have also incorporated into their much–loved hymns the magnificent handiwork of God. However, for Matthew Bridges and Godfrey Thring in their hymn: "Crown Him with Many Crowns," their encapsulation of God's handiwork has been expressed in a way that few have managed to achieve, which includes time and space in the way they describe the "Lord of the years" and His awesome power.

Their choice of words for the last verse, in particular the way that they describe God's creative acts, is an appropriate way to bring *Sign One* to its natural conclusion:

> Crown Him the Lord of Years,
> The Potentate of time
> Creator of the rolling spheres,
> Ineffably sublime;
> All hail, Redeemer, hail!
> For Thou hast died for me;
> Thy praise shall never, never fail,
> Throughout eternity.

THE SECOND SIGN

The birth of Jesus as observed in The Seven Feasts of the Lord. God's call to remembrance.

Having observed a lunar/solar link to the birth of Jesus, confirmed by the precision and nature of the universe (I know my reasoning is based on two consecutive years, not thirty-three and a half years, but it is the principle concerning the dates chosen for the Day of Atonement and for Passover that I believe to be valid), I then felt I needed to see something further in Scripture that would indicate when it was that Jesus was born. It was never my intention to *'Search the Scriptures'* to find something speculative to authenticate my initial discovery; rather, I wanted the Lord to provide additional confirmation from His Word that would indicate when it was that Jesus was born.

Having noted the correlation of solar years and lunar years, and having connected this detail to the birth and the death of Jesus, one day as I was leaving our home to take our dog for a walk I asked the Lord to show me again if the timing for Jesus' birth had been recorded in Scripture. Almost immediately I felt directed to consider one of David's psalms. It was as though the Lord was telling me where to look, but during my walk with Suzie I failed to see any connection, although I knew the Psalm well.

Later, as I read through the Psalm, I began to see that one thousand years before Jesus was born David appears to have been given detailed information about the timing of Jesus' birth.

Was this the word that I had asked the Lord for, and had He guided me to this particular Psalm in order for me to understand the relevance and the importance of the day chosen for His Son's birth?

Apart from what I had learnt about God's *'Rolling Spheres' (see Sign One)*, this was the first time that I had seen evidence in Scripture for when Jesus was born. Previously, like so many others, and over so many years, I was of the opinion that the Bible does not provide a date for Jesus' birth. I now realized that I had made a huge mistake in assuming this.

So obvious, yet also true, nobody can remember when they were born! To know our date of birth we can refer to our birth certificate to inform us of when the event took place. From when the Lord, I believe, gave me a Psalm to refer to, I have since viewed this Psalm as being Jesus' birth certificate.

Other books and searches on the Internet were not my source; I had not looked for their suggestions. I had prayed and the Lord in His love and His kindness had answered my prayer, therefore I give Him 100 percent of the credit.

What greatly surprised me was the date existed, in God's Word, long before Jesus was born.

Which Psalm?

In the Psalm I quote are listed *Seven Historical References* and *One Injunction.* There is also a reference that has a verb in the present tense with the seven *Historical References* and the one *Injunction* divided equally on either side, which means this additional reference is positioned at the Psalm's pivotal point. The other verbs used in this Psalm are all in the future tense; events which will happen at some future time, but which had not happened when the Psalm was first written.

Luke 22:44. "And being in agony, He (that is Jesus) prayed more earnestly. Then His sweat became like great drops of blood falling down to the ground." Moments before Jesus experienced this time of extreme personal crisis, He had prayed to His Father and asked: "Father, if it is your will, take this cup away from Me; nevertheless, not My will, but Yours be done." (Luke 22:42) Psalm 23:5. "My cup runs over." Psalm 23 is indeed the Psalm I had been prompted to consider. It was as I began to read David's much-loved Psalm that I saw *Seven Portraits* which describe the *Seven Feasts of the Lord.* The Feasts are listed in Leviticus 23, but it was as I read Psalm 23 that I saw how David describes the *Portraits of the Feasts* in the same order as the Feasts, commencing with Passover. Psalm 23 is, I believe, a very detailed Messianic portrait. Psalm 22 is a description of the life of Jesus; while Psalm 24 describes some of the aspects of His eternal qualities, therefore, to have Psalm 23 placed between the other two provides us with a stunning portrait in God's teaching to us about Jesus. The explanation is, I realize, a very basic one, yet basic explanations can be the most helpful as it means that everyone is able to understand its application. In explaining my understanding of Psalm 23, I trust you will see something of Jesus and appreciate how He is being portrayed.

The Passover Lamb

The first four stanzas of Psalm 23 are associated with God's provision of a Passover Lamb. When Jesus entered Jerusalem on "...a young donkey," the date was the tenth day of the Hebrew month Nisan. It was the same day of the same month as when the Children of Israel crossed the Jordan river to enter the Promised Land (Joshua 4:19). It was also the same day of the same month that the priests would have made their selection of a "...lamb without blemish" for Passover (Exodus 12:3). Four days later, on the fourteenth day of Nisan (Exodus 12:6), the Passover Lamb was sacrificed. It was also the same day that Jesus was crucified.

When John the Baptist saw Jesus coming towards him, he said of Him: "Behold! The Lamb of God who takes away the sin of the world!" (John 1:29).

When we think about Jesus and all that He fulfilled at Passover, as we now read the opening four stanzas of Psalm 23, it is Jesus we should be considering.

"The Lord is my shepherd;
I shall not want.
He makes me to lie down in green pastures;
He leads me beside the still waters."

When the hour came for Jesus to be glorified, He became troubled and said, "Now My soul is troubled, and what shall I say? 'Father, save Me from this hour'? But for this purpose I came to this hour. Father, glorify Your name." Then a voice came from Heaven, saying, "I have both glorified it and will glorify it again" (John 12:27–28). In the fifth stanza of Psalm 23, we read:

"He restores my soul."

When Jesus prayed to His Father, we are reminded that His *'Soul was troubled'* and was in need of comfort. It was then that the Father responded to encourage His Son with an audible voice that was heard from Heaven to restore His Son's soul.

The Feast of Unleavened Bread

When Passover and the first day of the Feast of Unleavened Bread were first instituted, they took place on the same day, from the eve of the 14th day of Nisan through to the eve of the 15th day (Exodus 12). Luke identifies the two feasts as being one. "Now the Feast of Unleavened Bread drew near, which is called Passover" (Luke 22:1). Ezekiel also refers to the two feasts as being one. "In the first month, on the fourteenth day of the month, you shall observe the Passover, a feast of seven days; unleavened bread shall be eaten" (Ezekiel 45:21).

At Passover and the Feast of Unleavened Bread there is an overlap, because two issues are to be remembered. First, Passover, a sacrifice to bring freedom. Second, Unleavened Bread, God's requirement for righteousness which will result in God saving a people for His own possession.

Leaven in the Bible is symbolic of sin and Pilate having examined Jesus in a similar way as the priests would have examined the Passover Lamb for any defects, proclaimed three times, "...I find no fault in Him" (John18–19). That Jesus was spotless, without sin, and that Pilate's assessment of Him took place on the day Jesus was to die, fulfilled both the Passover and Unleavened Bread requirements as first observed on the same day in the time of the Exodus. The 6th stanza of Psalm 23:

"He leads me in the paths (or cycles) of righteousness for His name's sake."

Righteousness and Unleavened Bread are synonymous and this is why leaven is removed from Jewish homes at the time of the Feast of Unleavened Bread.

At Calvary, Jesus gave Himself as a sinless sacrifice in order to proclaim victory over sin and death. And God's name was vindicated, by the righteousness and obedience of His Son, Jesus.

45

Passover

The next four stanzas (7–10) are again associated with the Passover theme. They portray how Jesus, God's chosen Passover Lamb, the *'Lamb of God'*, was made to suffer in order that the penalty of eternal justice and punishment for sin might be covered.

"Yea, though I walk through the valley
of the shadow of death,
I will fear no evil;
For You are with me;
Your rod and your staff, they comfort me."

From this description, it does seem entirely credible that these words do refer to the sufferings of Jesus at Passover, yet Jesus' confidence, which is in His Father, is assured, knowing that the Father will deliver Him from the "…shadow of death."

For Jesus, a cruel death was to be His experience, but He had no need to fear the consequence of death, or of evil, for God was with Him. Death, He knew, was part of God's plan, but then would come the fulfilment of the festival of Firstfruits.

The Feast of Firstfruits

The third feast in the cycle of the *Seven Feasts* is to celebrate the beginning of the barley harvest and this is why at the Feast of Firstfruits there is much rejoicing. The 11th stanza of Psalm 23.

"You prepare a table before me in the presence of my enemies."

By His resurrection Jesus has defeated sin and death (the two enemies that He came to conquer) and has thus prepared a table for celebration for those who put their trust in Him, and in the sight of those who opposed Him. We are invited to join Jesus in celebration and thanksgiving at the Feast of Firstfruits because sin and death have been defeated. "But now is Christ risen from the dead and has become the firstfruits of those who have fallen asleep" (1 Corinthians 15:20).

This reference in 1 Corinthians is an indication that the resurrection of Jesus took place at the festival of Firstfruits, for this feast was not celebrated on a particular day but was dependent on when the barley harvest commenced. The Feast of Firstfruits was observed on the first day of the week after the commencement of the barley harvest (Leviticus 23:10–14); therefore, when Jesus rose from the dead on the first day of the week, it was almost certain to have been on the occasion of the Feast of Firstfruits, that we might remember Him always with joy and thanksgiving.

The Feast of Weeks

Seven Sabbaths and one day later (fifty days) and the Feast of Weeks, which is sometimes known as the Feast of Latter Fruits, is held to celebrate the wheat harvest. In Matthew's gospel, Jesus is quoted as having said to His disciples: "The harvest truly is plentiful, but the laborers are few. Therefore pray the Lord of the harvest to send out laborers into His harvest" (Matthew 9:37–38). Today, we remember this feast as being "When the Day of Pentecost had fully come…" and the anointing oil of the Holy Spirit was poured out on the disciples and those who had become Jesus' followers, witnessed by the "…tongues, as of fire" that "…sat upon each of them" (Acts 2).

It was the fulfilment of what Jesus had promised His disciples He would do for them, after He had returned to the Father. Very significantly, the anointing of the disciples by the Holy Spirit took place at the Feast of Weeks, but also at Bethany: "A woman came to Him having an alabaster flask of very costly fragrant oil, and she poured it on His head as He sat at the table" (Matthew 26:7). Therefore, not surprisingly, for Jesus (and His promise to His disciples), the 12th stanza reads:

"You anoint my head with oil."

The Garden of Gethsemane

In the words of the 13th stanza from Psalm 23, I have not been able to see a connection to the *Seven Feasts of the Lord*, however, its inclusion comes at the psalm's pivotal point. Never underestimate the anguish that Jesus must have experienced in the Garden of Gethsemane. The word Gethsemane means *Olive Press*. The name of the garden and its ancient olive trees are a reminder of the process involved in extracting oil from olives. The process involves *crushing* the olives in order to extract every last drop of oil. Being *crushed* in Gethsemane is how Jesus must have felt as He contemplated His suffering on the eve of Passover, that He might become the fulfilment of the Passover sacrifice.

It was in Gethsemane that Jesus knelt down and prayed more earnestly, saying: "Father, if it is Your will, take this cup away from Me; nevertheless not My will, but Yours be done" (Luke 22:42). For Jesus, His cup did indeed *'run over'* when His "sweat became like great drops of blood falling down to the ground" (Luke 22:44). For Jesus, Gethsemane was a pivotal moment. The 13th stanza of Psalm 23 is also a pivotal moment.

"My cup runs over."

Some Bible commentators have said that the *Cup* that is referred to in Psalm 23 is a *Cup of Blessing* and not a *Cup of Sorrow*, which means it cannot refer to what Jesus experienced in Gethsemane. Partially, I agree, because I am persuaded that it is a *Cup of Blessing*, but at the same time it is also a *Cup of Sorrow.* Everything that Jesus did was done not for Himself but for others. Therefore, His *Cup of Sorrow* has become our *Cup of Blessing*. His righteousness redeems our unrighteousness. His death means for us life. His baptism by the Holy Spirit leads to our being baptized by the Holy Spirit.

His message of *Good News* is *Good News* for us. Because of Jesus' sacrificial death, it means we can be reborn to live a new kind of life, and so put away our old way of living.

Jesus was not crucified for any of His own wrongdoing, He died for others; He died for you and He died for me. For Jesus, His *Cup of Sorrow* which commenced in Gethsemane, heralded a time of extreme personal suffering, but for those who believe and put their trust in Him, His *Cup of Suffering* has resulted in their receiving His *Cup of Blessing.*

The Feast of Trumpets

The first day of the Hebrew Civil Year (the first day of the month Tishrei) was when the Feast of Trumpets was observed and two silver trumpets were blown as a "...memorial for you before your God; I am the Lord your God" (Numbers 10:10). The Feast of Trumpets is a *Day of Remembrance*, a *Day of Sounding,* and is known by Jewish people as *Rosh HaShanah.* According to Jewish tradition, this was when Abraham took his son Isaac up to Mount Moriah, the site on which Israel's temple would one day be built, and there Abraham laid his son on the wood he had prepared. As Abraham was about to slay his son, the angel of the Lord intervened and told Abraham not to kill Isaac. Abraham then took a ram that was caught by its horns in a thicket and offered it as a substitute sacrifice in place of his son, Isaac.

At the Feast of Trumpets, the sounding of the trumpet (nowadays the *Shofar*) is a reminder that if Israel is willing to respect, trust and obey God, then they will be saved from their enemies, saved from death; *Good News* indeed. The gospel is *Good News* because it includes the same provision, salvation from death, and Abraham and Isaac were the first to experience such a deliverance. As the 14th stanza from Psalm 23 so unequivocally states:

"Surely, goodness and mercy shall follow me."

In the book of Nehemiah we read that when Ezra stood on a wooden platform at the Water Gate in Jerusalem to read to the people from the book of the Law of Moses, he did so on the occasion of the Feast of Trumpets (Nehemiah 8:2). When Ezra read, the people stood, lifted their hands, bowed their heads, and worshiped. Nehemiah and Ezra then spoke to the people and said: "This day is holy to the Lord your God; do not mourn nor weep." For all the people wept when they heard the words of the law. Then he said to them, "Go your way, eat the fat, drink the sweet, and send portions to those for whom nothing is prepared; for this day is holy to our Lord. Do not sorrow, for the joy of the Lord is your strength." When the people heard the words spoken by Ezra on the occasion of the Feast of Trumpets, we are told that they rejoiced greatly, because they understood Ezra's words.

One of my most memorable experiences when visiting Jerusalem a few years ago was to walk through Hezekiah's tunnel, an underground aqueduct that flows from the Fountain Gate to the Water Gate. Carved through solid bedrock by Hezekiah's workers in 701 B.C., "This same Hezekiah also stopped the water outlet of Upper Gihon, and brought the water by tunnel to the west side of the City of David" (2 Chronicles 32:30). What a marvelous representation Hezekiah's tunnel is, with its life-giving water flowing from the Fountain Gate to the Water Gate? The Water Gate is the gate from where Nehemiah and Ezra spoke to the people on the occasion of the celebration of the Feast of Trumpets.

Writing prophetically, Zechariah recorded: "In that day a fountain shall be opened for the house of David and for the inhabitants of Jerusalem, for sin and for uncleanness" (Zechariah 13:1). Following Jesus' death, a Roman soldier took a spear and pierced His side and blood and water were released and so a channel was opened in Jerusalem whereby we can now receive "…a fountain of water springing up into everlasting life" (John 4:14). Then one of the elders said to John: "For the Lamb who is in the midst of the throne will shepherd them and lead them to living fountains of waters. And God shall wipe away every tear from their eyes" (Revelation 7:17).

What we read of in the book of Nehemiah is a wonderful description of the *Good News* of the gospel. The words, *'The Law of Moses'*, do not convey the true meaning of the word *Law*. The *Law of Moses* is not a negative concept; *Instruction* or *Teaching* are better, for it is when we understand God's instructions and His teaching that we can rejoice in God's *Goodness* and His *Mercy*.

This is what Nehemiah and Ezra communicated and it is also what Jesus taught. It is when we understand Jesus' teaching and its application that we can also *"...rejoice greatly"* as we stand, lift our hands, bow our heads, and worship Him.

When the Lord spoke to me about the birth of Jesus and suggested that I should consider Psalm 23, it was then that I saw something so compelling concerning the Feast of Trumpets. Silver is often referred to in the Bible as a sign of redemption and in the two silver trumpets that Moses made for God's people I see a very clear representation of the gospel.

The first silver trumpet I see as representing God's *Goodness* and it is confirmed in what Jesus said to the Pharisee, Nicodemus: "For God so loved the world that He gave His only begotten only Son..." (John 3:16). God's *Goodness* is represented in His *Love*, *"...for God is love"* (1 John 4:8).

The second silver trumpet I see as representing God's *Mercy* and is linked to God's love by what Jesus said both before and after His previously quoted statement: "...that whoever believes in Him should not perish but have eternal life" (John 3:15–16). *Mercy* is God's kindness.

In Hebrew, the word for *Mercy* is *Hesed and* Kevin Maxey, in his teaching about *Hesed*, has written:

> *"Translators have used a variety of words in their attempt to capture the complete meaning of Hesed. No one English word adequately embodies its full meaning. You will most often find it translated in your Bible with the words such as lovingkindness, mercy, goodness, or steadfast love. Although Hesed may seem completely foreign to many, most have heard of 'Hasidic' Jews. Hasidic is a form of our word Hesed, and describes those who aspire to practice and walk in Hesed. In the true Biblical sense of the word, we need to be a Hasidic people."*

Recalling Psalm 23, I have explained that God's *Goodness* is contained in His love; His *Mercy* is expressed in His kindness. In Psalm 136, God's goodness and His mercy are so comprehensively described that there is surely no equivalent rendering? Verse one: "Oh give thanks to the Lord, for He is good! For His mercy endures forever."

In Hebrew writing, repetition is quite common and in Psalm 136 (in which there are twenty-six verses) it states twenty-six times: "For His mercy *endures* forever." In the New King James Version of the Bible, the word *'endures'* is written in italics, to enhance its vividness and devotional quality. There is no limit to God's mercy. "Therefore know that the Lord your God, He is God, the faithful God who keeps covenant and mercy for a thousand generations with those who love Him and keep His commandments" (Deuteronomy 7:9).

I can think of no two words so profound in describing the gospel other than to say it is the *Good News* of God's *Goodness* and His *Mercy* – His *love* and His *kindness*. The apostle Paul wrote about this in his letter to Titus. "But when the kindness and the love of God our Saviour toward man appeared, not by works of righteousness which we have done, but according to His mercy He saved us, through the washing of regeneration and renewing of the Holy Spirit, whom He poured out on us abundantly through Jesus Christ our Saviour" (Titus 3:4–6). God's *Goodness* and His *Mercy* as described in Psalm 23 is illustrated by the two silver trumpets used at the time of the Feast of Trumpets. These two proclamations are the very essence of the gospel message which Jesus explained and demonstrated to His disciples.

The consequence of God's *Goodness* and His *Mercy* culminates in the remembrance which now follows: the sixth remembrance, which comes nine days later. It is the Day of Atonement, known by Jewish observers as *Yom Kippur*.

The Day of Atonement

"Then the angel said to them (the shepherds) 'Do not be afraid, for behold, I bring you good tidings of great joy which will be to all people. For there is born to you <u>this day</u> in the city of David a Saviour, who is Christ the Lord. And this will be the sign to you; you will find a Babe wrapped in swaddling cloths, lying in a manger'" (Luke 2:10–12).

Yes, the underlining is mine, but was *'this day'* in the angel's message the Day of Atonement? It could so easily have been so, I believe it was.

Once I had seen the context of Psalm 23, that it has such a striking resemblance to the *Seven Feasts of the Lord*, and the seven remembrances are repeated in the same order as they were first given by God to Moses (Leviticus 23), it then became clear that the 15th stanza of this psalm must correspond to the Day of Atonement, the holiest day of all in the Hebrew calendar; a most *Awesome Day*.

It was as I read the following words from Psalm 23 that I was persuaded that the day when Jesus was to be born (as with where He was to be born) had been prophesied. God's timing is especially important because God frequently embraces the nature and purpose of time for the events He has planned.

The longer we live (or the shorter it may be), for each one of us, Jesus included, our life span consists of the day from when we were born to the day when we will die. For the One who became the Son of Man, Jesus, the measurement of time for His life was so accurately defined. The 15th stanza:

"All the days of my life."

It was these six words from Psalm 23 that prompted me to see Jesus, from the day when He was born to the day when He died, indeed, 'all the days of His life'. New birth, either physical or spiritual, will always be linked to a relationship and God's gift of atonement enables all who believe in Jesus to live as God's children. And, if we have been born again "Beloved, now we are children of God; and it has not yet been revealed what we shall be, but we know that when He is revealed, we shall be like Him, for we shall see Him as He is" (1 John 3:2).

To understand the 15th stanza of Psalm 23 and how it is connected to the timing for Jesus' birth is to understand why God chose the date for the Day of Atonement; it is a *Sign*. The date for the Day of Atonement was not man's choice; God chose the date and He later informed His servant Moses of His decision.

I am convinced that God in His absolute sovereignty knew precisely when and where Jesus would be born, and also the time and place where He would later die. There is no reason why God should not have known about these times and places in advance, about when and where they would take place.

Israel's observance of the Day of Atonement

Now the Lord spoke to Moses... "This shall be a statute forever for you. In the seventh month, on the tenth day of the month, you shall afflict your souls, and do no work at all, whether a native of your own country or a stranger who dwells among you. For on that day the priest shall make atonement for you, to cleanse you, that you may be clean from all your sins before the Lord. It is a Sabbath of solemn rest for you, and you shall afflict your souls. It is a statute forever.

And the priest, who is anointed and consecrated to minister as priest in his father's place, shall make atonement, and put on the linen clothes, the holy garments; then he shall make atonement for the Holy Sanctuary, and he shall make atonement for the tabernacle of meeting and for the altar, and he shall make atonement for the priests and for all the people of the assembly. This is an everlasting statute for you, to make atonement for the children of Israel, for all their sins, once a year" (Leviticus 16:1, 29–34).

And Moses did as the Lord commanded him.

In the above passage, we read that in God's instructions to Moses concerning the Day of Atonement, His command was that for the Children of Israel it was to be an everlasting statute. The observance, which included detailed instructions, was to be observed once a year, as with a birthday.

Jesus, by His birth, His life and His death has fulfilled the unique work of the High Priest and that He did so by His appearance on the Day of Atonement is as rational as the morning light that dispels the darkness (Genesis 1:1–3). The principle and the pattern are identical.

What I noted that is so enlightening about the words "all the days of my life," and how it describes the life of Jesus (from when He was born to when He died), is how these words are first recorded in Genesis. In Genesis we read that: "...the Lord God said to the serpent: 'Because you have done this, you are cursed more than all cattle, and more than every beast of the field; on your belly you shall go, and you shall eat dust <u>all the days of your life</u>'" (Genesis 3:14). To Adam (verse 17), God said: "Cursed is the ground for your sake; in toil you shall eat it <u>all the days of your life</u>." The judgment of the serpent and of Adam who was tempted and who disobeyed, is similar to the description as found in Psalm 23, "...all the days of my life."

The consequences of sin are summarized using similar words as recorded in Psalm 23, and which Jesus, on behalf of others, was destined to experience from the day when He was born to the day He died.

The Day of Atonement now brings us to consider the final feast in the cycle of seven; it is The Feast of Tabernacles.

The Feast of Tabernacles

The Feast of Tabernacles completes the *Seven Cycles of Remembrance* and in the 16th stanza of

Psalm 23 we read:

"And I will dwell in the house of the Lord."

John 1:14. "And the Word became flesh and dwelt (or *Tabernacled*) among us, and we beheld His glory, the glory as of the only begotten of the Father, full of grace and truth." Jesus came to tabernacle (or *dwell*) among us. His dwelling on earth was temporary, as with the *Sukkot*, the temporary shelter that Jewish people construct for their personal use during the Feast of Tabernacles, until He had accomplished all that the Father had asked Him to do.

Jesus' objective was that we might become eternal with Him. Once He had completed His task, Jesus was able to return to the Father and to dwell "…in the House of the Lord" forever.

John 17:13, Jesus praying to His Father: "But now I come to You, and these things I speak in the world, that they may have My joy fulfilled in themselves." For all who believe in Jesus and have accepted Him as their Saviour, one day they will be able to *Tabernacle* with Him and they will then experience for themselves, fullness of joy and His eternal rest.

The Final Stanza

The final stanza of Psalm 23, the seventeenth, contains only one word but it expresses two sentiments. The first is related to how long the children of Israel were told to keep the *Seven Feasts of the Lord* and so the final stanza is connected to the feasts. God told the Children of Israel that they were to keep the feasts, as it states in Leviticus 23 and also in Psalm 23:

"Forever."

The second sentiment I see as relating to the promise that Jesus gave to those who put their trust in Him, *Everlasting Life*, which means, of course, *Forever*. Mary's *Song of Praise* when she *Magnified the Lord*, which like Psalm 23 contains seventeen stanzas (seventeen being the conclusion of adding seven to ten, the two numerals set aside for the Day of Atonement remembrance, the tenth day of the seventh month) and references to God's *Goodness* and His *Mercy*, ends with the same sentiment as found at the end of Psalm 23, *Forever.*

Is Psalm 23 a paraphrase?

For many years I had not understood the importance of the seven times, or periods, of Hebrew remembrance; therefore, I had not appreciated their significance. Having read Psalm 23 so many, many times, I had not realised that David's Psalm could be the key to understanding when Jesus was born.

Now that I have seen Psalm 23 as a paraphrase of Leviticus 23, I will never again view this Psalm as being anything other than a Messianic Psalm; a portrait that describes the birth, the work, and the death of Jesus, and His return to the Father for rest.

That David wrote this Psalm one thousand years before Jesus was born should not be problematic for anyone. Jesus said that the date when He will return is known only by His Father. God must also have known the date when Jesus would come the first time, the date of His birth.

These six words from Psalm 23, "All the days of my life" describe completely the life-span of the Day of Atonement sacrifice, be it a bull, a goat, or Jesus Himself, and it is now two thousand years from when Jesus was born to become God's gift for our atonement.

THE THIRD SIGN

The birth of Jesus as observed in the unfolding of God's Word and His servant Elijah – John the Baptist.

The first indication for the *Third Sign* for when Jesus was born I saw as being connected to *Darkness* and *Light*. "In the beginning…" "…darkness was on the face of the deep" (Genesis 1:1–2). Then God spoke. "…God said: 'Let there be light'" (verse 3). Night-time is a likely time when Jesus was born. "Now there were shepherds living out in the fields, keeping watch over their flock by night" (Luke 2:8). It was night-time when the angels informed the shepherds that Jesus had been born. In the beginning, when there was only darkness, God said: "Let there be light." Jesus said to the Pharisees (those living in spiritual darkness): "I am the light of the world. He who follows Me shall not walk in darkness, but have the light of life" (John 8:12).

The fulfilment of the words from Genesis chapter one is found in John 1:1–5. (Note that John starts his gospel in exactly the same way as Genesis commences.) "In the beginning was the Word, and the Word was with God, and the Word was God. He was in the beginning with God. All things were made through Him, and without Him nothing was made that was made. In Him was life, and the life was the light of men.   And the light shines in the darkness and the darkness did not comprehend it."

The second indication for the birth of Jesus in the *Third Sign* is linked to John the Baptist. "Behold, I send My messenger, and he will prepare the way before Me.   And the Lord, whom you seek, will suddenly come to His temple, even the Messenger of the covenant, in whom you delight. Behold He is coming, says the Lord of hosts." "Behold, I will send you Elijah the prophet before the coming of the great and dreadful day of the Lord. And He will turn the hearts of the fathers to the children, and the hearts of the children to their fathers, lest I come and strike the earth with a curse" (Malachi 3:1, 4:5–6). It is with these words that the Hebrew Bible ends.

The fulfilment of Malachi's prophecy is found in Matthew 11:7–15. Jesus is speaking:

"What did you go out into the wilderness to see? A reed shaken by the wind? But what did you go out to see? A man clothed in soft garments? Indeed, those who wear soft clothing are in king's houses. But what did you go out to see? A prophet? Yes, I say to you, and more than a prophet. For this is he of whom it is written: 'Behold, I send My messenger before your face, who will prepare Your way before You.'   Assuredly, I say to you, among those born of women there has not risen one greater than John the Baptist…" "…for all the prophets and the law prophesied until John. And if you are willing to receive it, he is Elijah who is to come. He who has ears to hear, let him hear!"

And in John 1:6–9 we read:

"There was a man sent from God, whose name was John. This man came for a witness, to bear witness of the Light, that all through him might believe. He was not that Light but was sent to bear witness of that Light. That was the true Light which gives light to every man coming into the world."

God's *Light* and His servant *John the Baptist* are what are spoken of at the beginning and at the end of the Hebrew Scriptures, and the two are closely related to each other in order that we might discover something particularly noteworthy concerning Jesus and the Day of His Birth.

The Apocrypha

When I first became a believer in Jesus, somehow, but I know not how, I became aware that there was a section of ancient Jewish writings known as the *Apocrypha* that Christians were not expected to read. The Apocrypha writings were not considered by early Christians to be a part of God's inspired Word and so had not been included in the Bible. I also learned that there was a period of about four hundred years between the closing of the Hebrew Bible Scriptures and the commencement of the New Testament period. It is a pity, but probably true, that most Gentiles know little about these four hundred years of Jewish history as it is an era that is not discussed because of its non-appearance in most Bibles. However, for Jewish people, it is an important part of their history and Jesus identified Himself with this period at the Feast of Hanukkah.

Hanukkah

Two days after I published my first booklet about the timing for the birth of Jesus (February 2011), in which I included the details of *Signs One* and *Two*, I purchased two Bible study books, both of which included a suggestion that Jesus may have been conceived at the time of the Jewish festival of Hanukkah. Both authors explained that this would mean that Jesus would have been born nine months later, at the Feast of Tabernacles. If both authors were correct in their understanding for when Jesus was conceived, and then later born, it meant I would have to rethink my own position that Jesus was born on the Day of Atonement.

It may be helpful if I explain a little of the background of Hanukkah. Although Hanukkah is not one of the *Seven Feasts of the Lord*, nevertheless Hanukkah is an important Jewish feast. Hanukkah dates back to the second century B.C., when the Syrian Antiochus IV Epiphanies desecrated the Jewish temple in Jerusalem by erecting a statue to the pagan god Zeus; he then sacrificed a pig in the temple. Antiochus also instructed that copies of the *Torah* – the five books of Moses – should be burnt.

The book of 1 Maccabees records that in 167 B.C., on the fifteenth day of the Hebrew month Chislev, Antiochus "...built the appalling abomination on the top of the altar of burnt offering." Then, "On the twenty-fifth day of each month, sacrifice was offered on the altar erected on top of the altar of burnt offering" (1 Maccabees 1:54 & 59).

The first time that this pagan sacrifice took place occurred on the twenty-fifth day of the Hebrew month Chislev in the year 167 B.C. The prophet Daniel had prophesied that this would happen and his prophecy was recorded. "And forces shall be mustered by him, and they shall defile the sanctuary fortress; then they shall take away the daily sacrifices, and place there the abomination of desolation" (Daniel 11:31). Of course such sacrilege was totally against all that God had intended for His people but the Children of Israel were powerless to prevent it from happening. Three years later, in the year 164 B.C. and under the leadership of a family who became known as the *Maccabees*, Antiochus and the Syrians were defeated and the temple was cleansed.

Then, "On the twenty-fifth of the ninth month Chislev (164 B.C.), they rose at dawn and offered a lawful sacrifice on the new altar of burnt offering which they had made. The altar was dedicated to the sound of hymns, zithers, lyres and cymbals, at the same time of the year and on the same day on which the Gentiles had originally profaned it" (1 Maccabees 4:52–54).

The return to authorized sacrifices and offerings would eventually become known as Hanukkah, or *'The Festival of Lights'*, because it was on this day that the Menorah lamps were relit. The priests, however, had only enough purified oil to last for one day, but Jewish tradition records that the Menorah lamps continued to burn for eight days before new oil could be pressed and purified.

The eight-day burning of the Menorah lamps from just one day's supply of oil is considered by Jewish people to have been a miracle.

Hanukkah is also known as the *'Feast of Dedication'* and we know that Jesus kept this feast because in John's gospel we read: "Now it was the Feast of Dedication in Jerusalem and it was winter. And Jesus walked in the Temple in Solomon's porch..." (John 10:22–23). So on what evidence have some biblical scholars suggested that Jesus may have been conceived at Hanukkah and that He was born nine months later, at the Feast of Tabernacles?

Dr. Richard Booker in his book *'Celebrating Jesus in the Biblical Feasts'* writes:

> *"It is possible that Jesus, God's true light, was conceived during Hanukkah, the Feast of Lights. According to Luke 1:5, Zacharias was a priest of the division of Abijah. Luke 1:8–11 says that Gabriel appeared to Zacharias when he was serving as a priest in the temple.*

Based on Rabbinic writings, the division of Abijah served as priests during the second half of the fourth month on the Jewish religious calendar. (See 1 Chronicles 24:1– 19). It was then late June when Elizabeth conceived John the Baptist. According to Luke 1:24–26, Mary conceived Jesus in the sixth month of Elizabeth's pregnancy. This means that Jesus was conceived during the latter part of the Jewish month Kislev, or late December on the Gentile calendar. Jesus was born nine months later, most likely during the Feast of Tabernacles. Forty days after Jesus was born, He was dedicated to His heavenly Father at the temple. It was there that Simeon said that Jesus was a light to bring revelation to the Gentiles, and the glory of Israel (see Luke 2:32). God's true light had come into the world to reveal His Father to us."

The second author of the two study books on the Jewish feasts that I purchased who suggested a similar position to that of Dr. Booker, is Jacob Keegstra, author of *'God's Prophetic Feasts'*.

Writing in 2006, Keegstra comments:

"We know that the priest Zacharias was serving in the Temple when the angel came to him to announce the birth of John the Baptist. Zacharias was assigned to the eighth group of

Abijah and served during the week of the 12th

Abijah and served during the week of the 12th Siwan. If we add the forty weeks for a normal pregnancy, we reach the 14th of Nisan; this means that John the Baptist was born at the beginning of Passover. According to Judaism, the herald of the Messiah is expected in a Passover night. Jesus was born six months after John; thus we reach the Feast of Tabernacles. Nine months before this feast, the Feast of Lights takes place, which means that Jesus was presumably conceived around the Feast of Lights or Hanukkah Feast. Was Jesus, the Light of the world, conceived at the Feast of Lights? ***"We do know that Jesus did not come by chance, but He came in the fullness of time, very consciously at God's time. Apparently, God's acts of salvation are inseparably bound up with His festivals."*** *(Bold emphasis added by the Author).*

With the prospect that my conviction that Jesus was born on the Day of Atonement being superseded by another opinion, and one put forward by two scholars with a greater knowledge of such things than myself (and my obtaining their writings only two days after my first booklet had been printed!), I decided I must do something practical; therefore, I carried out a two hundred and eighty day analysis.

Two hundred and eighty days is the widely accepted time period for the gestation of the human embryo, from the time of conception, through to the time of giving birth. Two hundred and eighty days is forty weeks. Therefore, beginning at midnight at Hanukkah (Wednesday, December 21ˢᵗ, 2011, in the Gentile calendar, and the 25ᵗʰ day of Kislev in the Jewish calendar, the date when the temple in Jerusalem had been rededicated), I counted forward two hundred and eighty days and discovered that the forty-week period culminates not at the Feast of Tabernacles as had been suggested by others, ___**but at exactly midnight on the Day of Atonement**___. Yes, and I do mean exactly!

In 2011, the date set aside for Hanukkah was Wednesday, December 21ˢᵗ, 2011. In 2012, the date set aside for the Day of Atonement was Wednesday, September 26ᵗʰ, 2012. (The Day of Atonement in the Hebrew calendar is always the tenth day of the seventh month.) The time interval between the two dates was precisely forty weeks! *Now that, surely, cannot be a coincidence, can it?* Until I had undertaken to consult the timing and the linkage within the Hebrew/lunar calendars and the ancient Jewish festivals, I was totally unaware that it was exactly forty weeks from Hanukkah (in 2011) to the Day of Atonement (in 2012).

This, a *Third Sign* for when Jesus was born, I discovered only after I had published my original booklet detailing *Signs One* and *Two*. Personally, I am extremely grateful to God for not having shown me this detail until after I had published the first two *Signs*, but that within two days after my first booklet had been printed, I purchased two study books – one written by an American, the other by a

Dutchman – and together they would assist me in discovering a *Third Sign.*

A few days later as I was cutting the lawns for one of my local pensioners, it occurred to me that in Paul's letter to the Galatians we read: "But when the <u>fullness of time</u> had come, God sent forth His Son, born of a woman, born under the law" (Galatians 4:4).

I do not believe that Mary the mother of Jesus, who having had to travel at the behest of the Romans from Nazareth to Bethlehem, a journey of approximately ninety miles, that when she had nearly reached the *full-term* of her pregnancy which the Holy Spirit had miraculously conceived within her womb, that she would have gone overdue by nearly a week. When it came to the birth of Jesus, I believe He was born on time, on the Day of Atonement, and that is exactly the period of time from the Feast of Hanukkah in one year to the Day of Atonement in the following year. "As for God, His way is perfect…" (Psalm 18:30). Always!

It is beyond my ability to explain how Jesus broke through the barriers of time and space to enter the womb of Mary, a virgin (Isaiah 7:14), at the precise time when an egg from one of her ovaries had just entered her uterus. For the fetus of our Saviour to then spend forty weeks in Mary's womb before being born as a man, the *Son of Man,* is incredible, but I believe it was so.

David, the psalmist, was perhaps the first person to comment on Mary's role in becoming the mother of Jesus. In one of the most famous Messianic psalms which details the life and sufferings of Jesus, David wrote: "But You are He who took Me out of the womb; You made Me trust while on My mother's breasts. I was cast upon You from birth. From my mother's womb You have been My God" (Psalm 22:9–10).

What Jesus has done for millions of His followers, including myself, and perhaps you, too, is also incredible. We who have been *Born Again*, and the evidence can be seen in changed lives, in the cosmos (time) and in history – *His story*.

Scientists say that they understand only 4 percent of the Cosmos, which means (if man knows the full extent of the heavens) that there exists 96 percent of the cosmos that they don't understand. One scientist has also observed: "The Cosmos is all that has been, all that there is, and all that will be." The reason why I took note of these words was because they reminded me of what was written about Jesus: "Jesus Christ is the same yesterday, today, and forever" (Hebrews 13:8).

The common definition of a straight line is that it is the shortest distance between two points; and time is also linear. Time for Jesus as far as this world is concerned is a line that can be traced from the dawn of creation (He was in the beginning) until the end of this world as we know it. Jesus' birth, to be followed by His death, unsurprisingly, was fixed by His Father to two moments of time in earth's history, and this is why an awareness of the time for Jesus' birth is so important, so beneficial.

When it comes to when and where Jesus was born, the writings of the Hebrew Bible and the New Testament provide us with a number of clues, which when taken seriously are so convincing, and is why as a result of God's gift of faith I do believe.

Can you imagine Mary on the Sabbath in a synagogue in Nazareth with the infant Jesus in her arms, as she together with the other women listen as one of the local Rabbis reads aloud Psalm 22, pondering within herself: *"That's my womb and my breasts that King David is referring to."* But then, as the Rabbi continues: "They pierced My hands and My feet; I can count all My bones. They look and stare at Me. They divide My garments among them, and for My clothing they cast lots" (Psalm 22:16–18). What would have been Mary's thoughts then? We do not know, but in describing Jesus and His birth and His death, Psalm 22 is as clear as that.

I have now referred to Jesus and the timing for His birth as seen in the *Cosmos* (1), in the *Seven Feasts of the Lord* (2), and in the unfolding of *God's Word* (3). This now leads us to consider the *Fourth Sign* for when Jesus was born. Its explanation and its application is one of the most basic reasons for deciding why the date for Jesus' birth was chosen in advance.

THE FOURTH SIGN

The birth of Jesus confirmed as God's High Priest.

Jesus having been chosen from the foundation of the world.

The *Fourth Sign* for the birth of Jesus on the Day of Atonement became apparent as I was reading the book of Hebrews. Of all the individual books in the Bible, Hebrews is probably my favorite because it explains the appointment of Jesus as being God's High Priest, God's personal representative. Hebrews can be read in less than an hour and I recommend reading it this way because it is the best way to understand what the writer of the book of Hebrews is describing.

Hebrews explains Jesus as fulfilling the role as God's chosen High Priest, the One who as Paul describes: "…is also risen, who is even at the right hand of God, who also makes intercession for us" (Romans 8:34). In His appointment as High Priest, Jesus did not enter God's presence with the blood of bulls and goats, but it was His own blood (His own life) that He offered as a sacrifice for our sin.

In Israel's ancient community, the role of the High Priest was crucial because his primary function was to act as God's representative. In doing so, his task was to perform a range of duties in order that the

Children of Israel might live according to God's instructions. Included in his many tasks was one that the High Priest was commanded to carry out which was of much greater importance than all of his other duties put together. On the Day of Atonement, the High Priest was told to remove and lay aside his regular priestly robes and to put on a simple linen garment before entering the Holy of Holies with the blood of the sin sacrifice. (It is also likely he removed his footwear.)

For his first visit into the Holy of Holies, the High Priest had to take the blood from a bull as a covering for his own sin. Afterwards, he took blood from one of two young goats as a covering for the sins of the people. The High Priest was told to sprinkle the blood of the sacrifice on the Mercy Seat, the covering of the Ark of the Covenant. The High Priest was instructed by God to carry out this procedure just once a year, on the Day of Atonement. See Leviticus chapter sixteen.

Tradition records that a length of cord was tied to one of the High Priest's ankles in case he was struck dead from having entered the Holy of Holies in an unworthy state. The cord would then enable the other priests to retrieve his body without having to enter the Holy of Holies themselves. Such was the respect and awe of entering God's presence on the Day of Atonement.

Of course, Israel's Day of Atonement procedure was only a temporary arrangement. A time would eventually arrive when God would send His Son, and men and women would no longer be dependent on a High Priest who was able to serve only in a limited and temporary capacity, until his death, when another priest would be appointed to replace him. Jesus is God's final High Priest (in Hebrew *Cohen Gadol*) and is the One never to be replaced. "But when the Messiah appeared as Cohen Gadol of the good things that are happening already, then, through the greater and more perfect Tent which is not man-made (that is, not of this created world) he entered the Holiest Place once and for all. And he entered not by means of the blood of goats and calves, but by means of his own blood, thus setting people free forever" (Hebrews 9:11–12). *(The Complete Jewish Bible).*

The recalling of goats and calves in this passage from Hebrews and of entering into "...the Holiest Place once for all," indicates that the writer is remembering what took place on the Day of Atonement and not the other occasions when the High Priest carried out his regular priestly service in the Tabernacle. In the book of Revelation we read: "...the temple of God was opened in Heaven, and the ark of His covenant was seen in His Temple" (Revelation 11:19). The Tabernacle, which included the Ark of the Covenant that Moses was told to make for the Children of Israel in the wilderness, was not an original but was a copy of that which already existed, in Heaven, so there is a clear link here with the Holy of Holies which formed part of the Tabernacle, and the temple of God in Heaven.

When reading about Jesus in Hebrews, the writer is stating that Jesus is God's High Priest. Previously, for all human High Priests, the most important duty they performed was when they entered the Holy of Holies on the Day of Atonement – the only day in each year they were allowed to do so. Consider now these words from Hebrews: "So also Christ did not glorify Himself to become High Priest, but it was He who said to Him: 'You are My Son, today I have begotten You'" (Hebrews 5:5).

What I discovered that is so riveting about this passage is how it is rendered in *The Complete Jewish Bible*. Remember the context; it is God choosing Jesus to be His High Priest, whose purpose was to enter the Holy of Holies. Therefore, it now becomes clear that this verse, and indeed all of Hebrews, is saying throughout that it is Jesus we should be "...looking unto, the author and finisher of our faith, who for the joy that was set before Him endured the cross, despising the shame, and has sat down at the right hand of God" (Hebrews 12:2).

This, then, is how Hebrews 5:5 is rendered in *The Complete Jewish Bible:* "So neither did the Messiah glorify himself to become Cohen Gadol (High Priest); rather, it was the One who said to Him, 'You are My Son; **today I have become Your Father.**'" *(Bold emphasis added).* Which is the *'today'* that God is referring to here? Fathers and mothers will remember (at least they should!) when it was that they first became parents; it was at the birth of their first child. A birth-day is always an important occasion when parents celebrate the result of them being joined together in marriage and in love that together they might bring into the world a new life. Imagine then the *day* referred to here by God when He announced prophetically, one thousand years before Jesus was born: *"You are my Son; today I have become Your Father."*

These words from Hebrews 5:5 (quoted also in Hebrews 1:5) are a direct quote from Psalm 2. The words are identical: "You are my Son; today I have become Your Father" (Psalm 2:7). Psalm 2 (as with Psalms 22, 23, and 24) is a Messianic Psalm; whenever we read it we should be thinking of Jesus. So when the psalmist says "…today," which day is he referring to?

I believe it to be the Day of Atonement, for this is when God told Moses that the High Priest was to enter the Holy of Holies and for him to make atonement (a covering) for the sins of God's people.

The timing for Jesus' birth was the opposite of what the High Priest was told to do on the Day of Atonement. The High Priest was told to enter the Holy of Holies to make atonement for the sins of the people and he carried out this duty on the tenth day of the seventh month, the Day of Atonement.

Jesus' birth heralded God becoming *Emanuel, God with us,* and His appearance as the Son of God (and also the Son of Man), was because He came from Heaven (the real Holy of Holies) and He did so to become a sacrifice at Passover, Passover occurring half a solar year after the Day of Atonement.

The principle for the Day of Atonement to occur half a solar year (180 degrees of a solar cycle) before Passover is one that is enshrined in Scripture. Twenty-five years after the Children of Israel were taken into captivity to Babylon, Ezekiel experienced: "…the hand of the Lord" being laid upon him and taking him in the power of the Spirit to Jerusalem.

The date God placed His hand upon His servant Ezekiel was the tenth day of the first month (Ezekiel 40:1–3). It was the day set aside for the priests to select "…a lamb without blemish" for Passover. As part of Ezekiel's vision (which is described over nine chapters, 40–48) and included in God's instructions to Ezekiel, there exists a pattern for worship that is to be followed on all of the Lord's appointed feast (or *Remembrance*) days.

Ezekiel was instructed: "But when the people of the land come before the Lord on the appointed feast days, whoever enters by way of the north gate to worship shall go out of the south gate; and whoever enters by way of the south gate shall go out by way of the north gate. He shall not return by way of the gate through which he came, but shall go out through the opposite gate. The prince shall then be in their midst. When they go out, he shall go out" (Ezekiel 46:9–10).

In His message to Ezekiel, God describes how His people are to approach Him. "Whoever enters by way of the North Gate to worship; should go out by the South Gate, and whoever goes in by way of the South Gate to worship; should leave by the North Gate." When God's people approach Him, Ezekiel is instructed that they should not leave God's presence by turning around and walking away from Him.

God commanded that from whichever direction His people entered His presence to worship, this was not an issue; essentially, it wasn't important. What was important was that God's people should not go out as they came in: *No turning back.* "Remember Lot's wife" (Luke 17:32)?

Surely, does it not still apply? Whatever our doubts, fears or weaknesses are when we draw near to God to worship Him, we are not to return to those things. God's people should always be looking to "...press toward the goal for the prize of the upward call of God in Christ Jesus" (Philippians 3:14) and not to return to those things, *those other things, those former things,* that will hold them back.

The process is mirrored in what is intended to take place from when we are born again to become God's children. The apostle Paul explains it as:

"When I was a child, I spoke as a child, I understood as a child, I thought as a child; but when I became a man I put away childish things. For now we see in a mirror dimly, but then face to face" (1 Corinthians 13:11–12).

My simple and very basic proposition for *Sign Four* is that on the Day of Atonement as the High Priest was entering the Holy of Holies in one direction, Jesus was entering this world from the opposite direction – from Heaven He came. When deciding where Jesus was to be born, Bethlehem was a pragmatic choice, for it was at Bethlehem that the Passover lambs were bred and set aside for Passover. "But you Bethlehem, in the land of Judah, are not the least among the rulers of Judah; for out of you shall come a Ruler who will shepherd My people Israel" (Matthew 2:6 in quoting Micah 5:2). And it was Bethlehem's shepherds (those who looked after the Passover lambs before their being chosen for sacrifice) who were the first to be told of Jesus' birth; He who was "The Lamb of God who would take away the sin of the world."

Equally pragmatic was when Jesus' birth should take place. In the setting aside of the Day of Atonement, many years prior to His birth – the only *Day* that carries such a designation – the Day of Atonement was such an obvious choice because it fulfils all that had been allocated to its purpose.

I believe that Jesus' birth is one of the most reliable events in history, because of what had existed previously in Israel's history as a type. That God should send His Son and that His birth should be linked to the timing for when the earthly (temporary) High Priest entered God's presence in the Tabernacle, is so rational because it fits the whole concept (*Pattern*) of that which was observed earlier by those chosen to be a High Priest.

The High Priest's entrance was imperfect, because of man's frailty and his propensity to commit sin. Only Jesus could provide a perfect solution to man's problem of sin and that He entered this world by arriving on the only day in the Hebrew/lunar calendar that makes any sense is now so obvious. Conceptually, when considering the seven times of remembrance in the Hebrew calendar, there is no other day that is so suitable for Jesus' birth other than on the Day of Atonement.

Therefore, when considering the original concept for the Day of Atonement, Jesus would have known that besides visiting Jerusalem to observe this day (His birthday?) of remembrance, in Bethlehem He had been born of God to become its fulfilment. It is inconceivable that Jesus would have ignored the Day of Atonement for He knew He had been appointed by His Father to act as our High Priest.

Just a few hours before He was crucified, Jesus said to His disciples: "I came forth from the Father and have come into the world. Again, I leave the world and go to the Father" (John 16:28). His words are a clear statement referring both to His birth and His approaching death. It is unimaginable that the date for Jesus' birth was not important to His Father (or to Himself), for God knew that from the day when

He was born He was destined to become a High Priest and that His work would commence from when He reached age thirty (Numbers 4:3). Three and a half years later (Daniel 9:27), Jesus would become our Passover sacrifice, and when God witnessed the death of His Son, He promised that for those who believed and trusted in Him, they would not be condemned to an eternal death and separation from God. Jesus came to bring us freedom; freedom from being slaves to sin and sin's consequence.

"Seeing then that we have a great High Priest who has passed through the heavens, Jesus the Son of God, let us hold fast our confession. For we do not have a High Priest who cannot sympathize with our weaknesses, but was in all points tempted as we are, yet without sin. Let us therefore come boldly to the throne of grace, that we may obtain mercy, and find grace to help in time of need" (Hebrews 4:14–16).

~ ~ ~

Within the Veil, I now would come,
Into the Holy Place to look upon Thy face,
I see such beauty there,
No other can compare,
I worship Thee my Lord,
Within the Veil.

(Author: Ruth Dryden)

THE FIFTH SIGN

The birth of Jesus as seen by what is good.

Truth unchanged from the dawn of time.

In *Sign Two* I quoted Professor Marcus du Sautoy who has said: "My big thesis is that although the world looks messy and chaotic, if you translate it into the world of numbers and shapes, patterns emerge and you start to understand why things are the way they are. It's numbers that dictate how the world must be."

Numbers and patterns are existent in both the Hebrew alphabet (Hebrew letters have a numeric value) and the Hebrew Scriptures, to explain God's plans for His people involving His Son Jesus. Therefore, a basic grasp of the use of numbers and patterns (including cycles of time) as they appear in the Bible will result in a greater understanding of God's purposes for His people as made known through His Word.

Having completed *Four Signs* for Jesus' birth, and in doing so linked each of the *Signs* to the Day of Atonement, I concluded that my task was complete. Later, however, as I considered the numerical order of the *Seven Feasts of the Lord*, I began to question what was the significance of the way the feasts had been arranged? Was there an order (or *pattern*) to the feasts, and if so, why? As I considered the order of the feasts, in my mind I became focused. It was obvious that the pattern for the feasts had been ordained by God, not chosen by Israel, but why had God ordained Israel's feasts in this particular way?

On Wednesday, January 23, 2013, at about 4:30 p.m., I asked my wife if she would like a cup of tea, and her having replied, *"Yes, please,"* I filled the kettle and switched it on. Initially, there was only silence, but silence, I've learned, can be precious, because it enables the Holy Spirit to speak to us without interruption.

In the quietness of the moment, brief though it was, I felt prompted to consider Genesis chapter one; but then, as the kettle began to boil and to protest, the silence was broken. However, the silence had been sufficient, and in turning to Genesis chapter one my thoughts went back to the dawn of time and the well-known account of creation, which in turn would lead me to consider a *Fifth Sign* for Jesus' birth being linked to the Day of Atonement.

It was as I read that I began to see that the account of creation has a striking resemblance to the *Seven Feasts of the Lord*. But it was not that I had recalled any teaching on this subject, not so, but my mind was open, because two days earlier I had asked the Lord to show me if there was something still missing in my understanding about why the date chosen for the Day of Atonement was so significant, so important.

The explanation which follows is as a result of my asking the Lord to help me to understand if the birth of Jesus was linked to other events in His Word. What I did not expect was to learn of a pattern in creation that culminated in God making man in His own image.

The Genesis account of creation and the miraculous birth of Jesus are, for some, two issues that may appear to be wrapped in mystery, but they are two issues that have a resonance of certainty embedded in their detail. Having been prompted to consider Genesis chapter one, and having seen this detail as an additional *Sign* for the timing for Jesus' birth, I am now able to view the events of creation as a mosaic of epic proportions. Genesis chapter one depicts Jesus better than any artistic impression; it is the world's first and finest portrait, the greatest non-fiction story ever told, and it is all about Him.

Day One

"In the beginning God created the heavens and the earth. The earth was without form and void; and darkness was on the face of the deep. And the Spirit of God was hovering over the face of the waters. Then God said: 'Let there be light'; and there was light. And God saw the light, that it was good; and God divided the light from the darkness. God called the light Day, and the darkness He called Night. So evening and morning were the first day" *(Genesis 1:1–5).*

The events of *Day One* are perhaps not as simple as

they may at first appear. For example, what is the nature of the *Light* that is described here? Clearly, it is not the light of the sun, for the sun does not feature until the fourth day. Might this be a way of describing not only what took place in the beginning, but also what takes place at the end of the ages, when God's Holy City, the New Jerusalem, has "…no need of the sun or the moon to shine in it, for the glory of God illuminated it. The Lamb is its light" (Revelation 21:23)?

Also, could it be a way of describing a conflict between the forces of light (God) and the forces of darkness (Satan), when the *Lamb of God* who is the *Light of God*, triumphs over the forces of darkness; sin and death? This might explain why days in the Hebrew Bible – and in Jewish life today – begin in the evening (the night) and extend into morning (the day).

Whatever the explanation (and we may not know the full explanation until it is fully explained to us, by God), Genesis introduces us to God and how He is represented by *Light*, and also to Jesus, who is *'The Light of the World'*.

Consider now the chronological order of the *Seven Feasts of the Lord* (Leviticus 23). Passover is described as being the *first* of the *Seven Feasts* and the numerical value of *one* is that it indicates a state of *Unity*. God is also represented by *one*, for God is *One*. Prior to when the Children of Israel were delivered from slavery in Egypt, Moses was told to instruct the people to select a "one-year-old male lamb on the tenth day of the first month." The lamb was to be killed on the fourteenth day, the day of preparation for the Passover, and its blood was to be smeared on the doorposts and the lintel of each house, as a *Sign to the Lord* that the house was occupied by God's chosen people, and that when God passed over Egypt "...at midnight" (Exodus 12:29), the household would be spared God's judgment. The one-year-old lamb was *A Lamb for a Family*.

When the Children of Israel crossed the river Jordan to enter the Promised Land, they did so on the same day, the tenth day of the first month, the day when they were told to select a one-year-old male lamb for the keeping of Passover (Joshua 4:19). On this occasion, now that the Children of Israel were entering the Promised Land, the Passover Lamb became *A Lamb for a Nation*.

When Jesus entered Jerusalem, again on the tenth day of the first month, the same day the Passover Lamb was to be chosen, Jesus was about to become at Passover *A Lamb for the World*. The Lamb of God, God's only Son, was to be the One who would take away the sin of the world. (John 1:29).

On each of these three occasions, the Passover Lamb was to bring first a family, then a nation, then the world into a covenant relationship with God. The purpose of Passover is to enable God's people to be saved, so that when God observes the blood

("For the life of the flesh is in the blood..." (Leviticus 17:11), God promises to *pass-over* His people and to save them. The uniqueness of who Jesus is and His willingness to become the only sacrifice which can take away sin, points us to *Day One* when God said: "Let there be light." Jesus is God's Light and was the future fulfilment of what God established on *Day One*.

Jesus died at Passover because He was appointed as the *One* who could remove sin. Peter the Apostle spoke of this when he said: "Nor is there salvation in any other, for there is no other name under Heaven given among men by which we must be saved." (Acts 4:12). And in John's gospel we read, Jesus speaking: "And now O Father, glorify Me together with Yourself, with the glory which I had with You before the world was." (John 17:5). Jesus and the Father are *ONE* and it was at Passover, the *First* of the Seven Feasts, that God "...gave His only begotten Son..." as a sacrifice for sin. (John 3:16). *(Author's underlining)*

Having noted how *'One'* in Hebrew thought conveys the idea of unity and that Passover is the first of the *Seven Feasts* as described in Leviticus 23, then as we read the account of what took place on *Day One* we note that God said: "Let there be light" – God's first command and on that first day. As a result of God's command, what had existed previously, namely darkness, now there was light, and the light appeared before the Sun and the Moon appeared on *Day Four*.

In John's first letter we read that: "…God is light and in Him is no darkness at all." (1 John 1:5). What is described as having taken place on *Day One* is an indication of one of the virtues of the Divine nature, that of light.

When light made its first appearance, it displaced the darkness, because God is not characterized by the darkness. Jesus said: "I am the light of the world. He who follows me shall not walk in darkness but shall have the light of life" (John 8:12).

Recalling how Jesus is being referred to symbolically on *Day One* in Genesis, then shortly before 'The light of the world' was about to be <u>extinguished at Passover</u>, Jesus explained to His disciples the importance of this attribute: "A little while longer the light is with you. Walk while you have the light, lest darkness overtake you; he who walks in darkness does not know where he is going. While you have the light, believe in the light, that you may become sons of light" (John 12:35–36).

Also: "Then Jesus cried out and said, 'He who believes in Me, believes not in Me but in Him who sent Me. And he who sees Me sees Him who sent Me. I have come as a light into the world, that whoever believes in Me should not abide in darkness' " (John 12:44–46).

When Jesus spoke these words He had only recently told His disciples that His final hour was near. (John

12:23 & 27). Earlier, John tells us: "...His hour had not yet come" (John 8:20). But with the approach of Passover, Jesus knew He was about to die; His hour (*His Time*) had finally come. And what was it that took place as Jesus suffered and died? "...there was darkness over all the earth until the ninth hour" (Luke 23:44). It was a return to the darkness that had existed in the beginning, prior to God saying: "Let there be light". The death of Jesus at Passover completed the first stage in the cycle of God's *Seven Remembrances*, and His death brought about a return to the darkness, but only briefly.

The darkness that occurred as Jesus suffered and died lasted for just three hours. When we come to *Day Three* we will be thinking about the resurrection of Jesus and what took place three days after He died at the time of the festival of Firstfruits. At the time of Jesus' death, this brief period of darkness was an indication that such darkness, although real and a darkness that was feared by those who witnessed this phenomenal occurrence, thankfully, it was not a darkness that would last forever. The Scriptures clearly inform us that Jesus was chosen by God to destroy the works of darkness and man's separation from God, caused when man first sinned.

As Jesus died, it is quite understandable why the darkness returned, even though the sun and the moon must surely have remained in their pre-ordained positions? In Genesis, the events of *Day One* explain Calvary at the time of Passover, but it was a reversal of the typology. As the "Light of the world" was being "…cut off from the land of the living" (Isaiah 53:8), so the darkness returned to cover the earth. The terminology is similar to when an electrical power failure occurs and a community is *Cut Off* from the electricity supply and plunged into darkness.

Philip, one of Jesus' disciples, was puzzled as to the relationship Jesus had with the Father and so he asked Jesus: "Lord show us the Father, and it is sufficient for us." Jesus replied: "Have I been with you so long, and yet you have not known Me, Philip? He who has seen Me has seen the Father; so how can you say, 'Show us the Father'? Do you not believe that I am in the Father, and the Father in Me?" (John 14:8–10). Jesus is *One* with the Father, theirs is a relationship of unity. Note His words at the Feast of Dedication (Hanukkah, the Festival of Light): "I and My Father are one" (John10:30). For God and for Jesus, each possess the same attribute, that of *'Light'*.

Because of Israel's slavery in Egypt, and our slavery to commit sin – "Jesus answered them, 'Most assuredly, I say to you, whoever commits sin is a slave of sin" (John 8:34) – the Passover Lamb was slain, first for a family, then for Israel, and finally for the world. Passover is a symbolic type; it was to allow the Children of Israel to go free from their slavery and to enter the Promised Land. The last Passover sacrifice, Jesus, is God's way of setting us free from being slaves to sin and to receive His promised inheritance, that of Heaven. For Jesus, it was the fulfilment of the Exodus symbolism. Jesus' *One-Ness*, His uniqueness, has also been confirmed in Scripture as Him being God's only Son. He who is the Light of the world was briefly, at the time of Passover, extinguished, Passover being the *First* of the *Seven Appointed Times* as explained by what took place on *Day One*.

Day Two

"Then God said, 'Let there be a firmament in the midst of the waters, and let it divide the waters from the waters.' Thus God made the firmament, and divided the waters which were under the firmament from the waters which were above the firmament; and it was so. And God called the firmament Heaven. So the evening and the morning were the second day" (Genesis 1:6–8).

The number *Two* in Scripture speaks to us of *Separation*, or *Division*, and here in Genesis we read that on *Day Two* God divided the waters by means of a firmament and the firmament He called *Heaven*. There exists, as Jesus has explained, a distinction between that which He called *Heaven* and that which He called *Hell*. Jesus came to enable us to enter Heaven and we can do so by taking upon ourselves (providing we repent of our sin), His gift of righteousness. Therefore, the application and an understanding of the Feast of Unleavened Bread, the *Second Appointed* Time, makes it clear that we can associate this feast with what took place on *Day Two* in creation. It was the division of the firmament and the place in between God refers to as being *'Heaven'*.

When God made man He gave him two choices, to obey or not to obey, which resulted in two spiritual destinies. Man's choice related to what God had prepared on *Day Two*. It is what Jewish people are told to remember when they keep the Feast of Unleavened Bread. They are commanded to remove all *Leaven* from their homes because *Leaven* is symbolic of sin; *it permeates the all*, which is also the consequence of disobedience. James taught that if we stumble in one aspect of God's law then we are guilty of breaking all of the law's requirements (James 2:10).

Because God required the Children of Israel to make a distinction between *Unleavened Bread* and *Leavened Bread*, illustrating the polarization of *Righteousness* and *Unrighteousness* – by definition the two cannot co-exist – explains why the Feast of Unleavened Bread is the *Second Appointed Time* and also explains the division that God performed on *Day Two*. God divided the waters, as He later demonstrated when the Children of Israel departed from Egypt.

The parting of the waters on *Day Two* and of the Red Sea for the Children of Israel to leave Egypt and their slavery behind, is also a picture of baptism. When a believer repents of their sin and is then lowered into the water to be baptised "…for the remission of sins" (Acts 2:38), the water is divided, thus enabling him/her to rise in newness of life and to be set free from being a slave to sin.

In His Sermon on the Mount, Jesus spoke of two gates: "Enter by the narrow gate; for wide is the gate and broad the way that leads to destruction, and there are many who go in by it. Because narrow is the gate and difficult is the way which leads to life, and there are few who find it" (Matthew 7:13–14).

In Paul's teaching to the early church, when writing to the church in Corinth, Paul wrote: "For He (that is God) made Him (Jesus) who knew no sin to be sin for us, that we might become the righteousness of God in Him" (2 Corinthians 5:21). Again, two ways.

These two quotations illustrate how Jesus separates or divides, because Jesus who is righteous was willing to take upon Himself our sin that we might become righteous through Him. The second feast, Unleavened Bread, explains why Jesus had to die, that we might be cleansed and forgiven.

What God established on *Day Two* and what took place during the Feast of Unleavened Bread, speaks to us of two ways: the way to life righteousness and the way to death sinfulness.

Jesus' objective and His accomplishment was that the firmament which came into existence on *Day Two*, *'Heaven'*, might become our inheritance.

Day Three

Following the death of Jesus, His bodily resurrection took place on the third day and was in line with what took place on the third day of the first week. The following events took place *before the sun and the moon appeared on Day Four.*

"Then God said, 'Let the waters under the heavens be gathered together into one place, and let the dry land appear'; and it was so. And God called the dry land Earth, and the gathering together of the waters He called Seas. And God saw that it was good. Then God said. 'Let the earth bring forth the grass, the herb that yields seed, and the fruit tree that yields fruit according to its kind, whose seed is in itself, on the earth'; and it was so. And the earth brought forth grass, the herb that yields seed according to its kind, and the tree that yields fruit, whose seed is in itself according to its kind. And God saw that it was good. So the evening and the morning were the third day" (Genesis 1: 9–13).

Before *Day Three*, "The earth was without form and void; and darkness was on the face of the deep" (Genesis 1:2). In the beginning, the earth had no form and no substance, so that when God began His working week, His objective was to create life on a sphere where prior to His creativity there was no life, no order, nothing. In a desert region where nothing appears to grow, when a rare thunderstorm occurs, suddenly new life can begin to appear. In the Sahara Desert there is a plant which is known as

'The Resurrection Plant' which can give the appearance of being completely dead because it has no roots and is blown about by the desert winds; however, when it rains, its seeds, which are cocooned in pods, fall into the ground and within days new shoots will begin to appear as new plants start to grow.

Shortly before Jesus raised Lazarus from the dead, Jesus said to Martha: "I am the resurrection and the life, He who believes in Me, though he may die, he shall live" (John 11:25). Later, having died Himself, Jesus confirmed He was the resurrection by rising from the dead on the third day. And, His resurrection must have taken place on the occasion of the third Jewish feast, the Feast of Firstfruits, for Firstfruits is what took place on *Day Three*: "...the earth brought forth grass, the herb that yields seed according to its kind, and the tree that yields fruit, whose seed is in itself according to its kind. And God saw that it was good." *Firstfruits?*

Jesus said: "Most assuredly, I say to you, unless a grain of wheat falls into the ground and dies, it remains alone; but if it dies, it produces much grain" (John 12:24). Was Jesus thinking here of Himself, knowing that when He died He would be placed in an earthen tomb, only to rise again after three days in newness of life (as a seed germinates?) in order to bring to the Father a harvest of souls?

It is possible that some readers may have doubts about the Biblical account of creation as described in Genesis chapter one, and in particular the appearance of grass, herbs and trees that yielded fruit (Firstfruits) and which took place on *Day Three*, which was before the sun and the moon (and the stars also) appeared on *Day Four*.

Before I explain what could be taking place on *Day Three*, compare Genesis on *Day One* when God said: "Let there be light", with Revelation 22:5. "There shall be no night there. They need no lamp nor light of the sun, for the Lord God gives them light."

When considering what took place on *Day Three*, these events are not so remarkable as they point to the third day, after Jesus' death and resurrection, and the Jewish festival of Firstfruits.

For a botanist, what occurred on *Day Three* may seem very unlikely, because of the need for photosynthesis. Photosynthesis is the building up of complex compounds in the chlorophyll process which can only take place by means of the energy provided by light, usually the sun. Therefore, how should we respond to the events of *Day Three*? *Day Three's* events are not so unlikely, not if they are related to Jesus.

The Gospels inform us that when Jesus died, when He was *"Cut Off"* from the land of the living, it became dark, and the darkness remained for three hours. The limit of darkness to just three hours could have been an indication that although Jesus

99

had died, *to have extinguished the Light of the World* would not result in an enduring darkness, with little or no hope, but that when Jesus rose from the dead a type of photosynthesis occurred in which Jesus promised to give life to all who seek it. Jesus said: "I am the light of the world. He who follows Me shall not walk in darkness but have the light of life." (John 8:12). This, I believe, is what the miracle of the *Third Day* is suggesting.

The seemingly impossible events of *Day Three* (which took place *before* the appearance of the sun and the moon on *Day Four* which control *Time* and the *Seasons*), are perhaps not so remarkable when put into the context of them having been fulfilled by Jesus, He who is the *'Light of the World'* and who was not *Cut-Off* forever, but who lives forever to make intercession for us.

The number *Three* in Scripture is widely recognized as being the number for *Resurrection* and is confirmed in why Jesus was to remain in the tomb for three days and three nights, before He rose from the dead after the three days.

Three is also a *Sign* of *Divine Perfection*, and Jesus spoke of His resurrection as being similar to when Jonah was in the belly of the great fish for "…three days and three nights; so will the Son of Man be three days and three nights in the heart of the earth" (Matthew 12:40). The reference by Jesus to His resurrection was the only *Sign* that Jesus was prepared to give to those who asked Him for a

Sign, yet surely it was the most appropriate *Sign*? Hindsight, I know, can make all the difference.

Jesus, in recalling the story of Jonah who was thrown into the sea, followed by Jonah's entombment for three days and three nights in the belly of the great fish, before being vomited on to dry land, was to be replicated by Jesus' own entombment in the heart of the earth, followed three days and three nights later by His resurrection, the sea and the earth having been made on day three.

And Jesus' disciples, who were later prepared to die for Him, their willingness to suffer for Jesus proves beyond all reasonable doubt that after the three days Jesus did indeed rise from the dead and then appeared to His disciples. Would the disciples have been prepared to die for Him if they thought Jesus might have been fraudulent; a man like they?

For those who questioned Jesus about His Divine credentials, they would have found guidance by referring to the *Torah* – the five books of Moses. Here we read that after the Children of Israel had crossed the Red Sea (a figurative way of describing the efficacy of Jesus and how division provides a way of escape from both slavery and sin), that they journeyed for three days without finding water. In their three days' journey, the Children of Israel became a thirsty people, so that when they eventually found water but it was bitter, they complained to Moses. In his desperation Moses prayed and in His response God showed Moses a tree. Moses took the tree and cast it into the bitter water, which then became sweet, allowing the people to drink and to quench their thirst.

Does this tree which God provided for His people after *three days and three nights* of wandering in the desert – God made the trees on the third day – not speak to us about the *Cross of Wood* on which Jesus died, the One who provides "…living water" (not bitter water) which will become: "…in him a fountain of water springing up into everlasting life" (John 4:10 & 14)?

At the end of the ages when Jesus reigns and there is "…a pure river of water of life, clear as crystal, proceeding from the throne of God and of the Lamb" (Revelation 22:1), it is described as being the time when: "And the Spirit and the bride say 'Come!' And let him who hears say, 'Come!' And let him who thirsts come. Whoever desires, let him take the water of life freely" (Revelation 22:17).

In the book of Isaiah, this theme is commented upon as we read: Thus says the Lord… "Ho! Everyone who thirsts, come to the waters; and you who have no money, come buy and eat. Yes, come, buy wine and milk without money and without price" (Isaiah 55:1). God's exhortation goes on to say: "For My thoughts are not your thoughts, nor are your ways My ways," says the Lord. "For as the heavens are higher than the earth, so are my ways higher than your ways, and My thoughts than you thoughts" (verses 8 & 9). In keeping to the theme of what took place on the third day and the resurrection of Jesus, this record continues: "…and all the trees of the field shall clap their hands. Instead of the thorn shall come the cypress tree, and instead of the brier shall come up the myrtle tree; and it shall be to the Lord for a name, for an everlasting sign that shall not be cut off" (Isaiah 55:12–13). Is God saying here that because Jesus will not again be *"Cut Off"*, never again die, that even the trees will rejoice, they *"shall clap their hands"*, they that were made on the third day and Jesus who rose on the third day?

Day Four

In *Sign One* I referred to the earth, the moon and the sun and that within this tripartite relationship, earth's journey through the cosmos can be traced. Created by God's divine command, the harmony that is shared by these three elements appears to confirm that Jesus is indeed the focus of these first seven days. Therefore, what God created on the *Fourth Day* – the sun and moon to act as *'Signs'* and *'Times'* – is part of God's work and is why the observance of the *Fourth* of the *Seven Feasts*, the Jewish *Feast of Weeks*, was ordered. The *Feast of Weeks* is when Israel's spiritual leaders were told to return thanks to God for their annual wheat harvest.

"Then God said, 'Let there be lights in the firmament of the heavens to divide the day from the night; and let them be for <u>signs and seasons, and for days and years</u>; and let them be for lights in the firmament of the heavens to give light on the earth;'

and it was so. Then God made two great lights; the greater light to rule the day, and the lesser light to rule the night. He made the stars also. God set them in the firmament of the heavens to give light on the earth, and to rule over the day and over the night, and to divide the light from the darkness. And God saw that it was good. So the evening and the morning were the fourth day" (Genesis 1:14–19).
(Author's underlining)

Earlier, I explained the importance of the sun, which gives light and heat during the day, and the moon and the stars, which give light and beauty at night, and how the sun, the moon and the earth's tilt control the earth's seasons. It is the sequential order of the seasons that are necessary for the harvest and the *Fourth Day* of creation began the order of events that determine the long-term viability of life on planet earth, particularly the harvest, for without it man could not survive. The harvest is God's provision and for the harvest to flourish there is a need for the four seasons: *winter*, *spring*, *summer,* and *autumn*. Each of the *four seasons* has a role to play in ensuring the harvest and the conditions required were first established on *Day Four*.

Jesus said: "The kingdom of God is as if a man should scatter seed on the ground, and should sleep by night and rise by day, and the seed should sprout and grow, he himself does not know how. For the earth yields crops by itself: first the blade, then the head, after that the full grain in the head. But when the grain ripens, immediately he puts in the sickle, because the harvest has come" (Mark 4:26–29).

Jesus portrayed the kingdom of God as being like a harvest field, and the harvest is made possible by what took place on the *Fourth Day*, the emergence of the sun and the moon in particular – and "He made the stars also" (Genesis 1:16).

The fourth feast in the cycle of seven is the Feast of Weeks, the wheat harvest, and was when Jesus sent the Holy Spirit to the disciples in Jerusalem in order for them to become His workers in the harvest field of the world which God created on *Day One*. Jesus said to His disciples: "The harvest is truly plentiful, but the laborers are few. Therefore pray the Lord of the harvest to send out laborers into His harvest" (Matthew 9:37–38).

The famous *'Great Commission'* of Jesus to His disciples was for them to "Go into all the world (the harvest field) and preach the gospel to every creature. He who believes and is baptized will be saved; but he who does not believe will be condemned." (Mark 16:15–16).

Regarding God's promises to Israel, and in particular to His servant David, God said: "Once I have sworn by My holiness: I will not lie to David: His seed shall endure forever, and his throne as the sun before Me; it shall be established forever like the moon, even the faithful witness in the sky" (Psalm 89:35–37). Three thousand years after God assured David of His promises, the sun and moon remain as God's faithful witnesses, and they were made on *Day Four*, four linking the *Four Seasons* and the fourth feast, the Feast of Weeks, which is held annually to celebrate the wheat harvest.

The number *Four* is understood by Hebrew scholars to be associated with that which pertains to God's creative works; the four seasons, the four points of the compass (north, south, east and west), the four winds, etc,. When Jesus sent the Holy Spirit on the occasion of the Feast of Weeks, the fourth feast (in Greek *Pentecost*), it was because God's work on earth was incomplete; the Gospel had still to be preached to the ends of the earth.

To enable the Great Commission to proceed, Jesus promised His disciples: "Behold, I send the Promise of My Father upon you; but tarry in the city of Jerusalem until you are endued with power from on high" (Luke 24:49).

Interestingly, when Jesus' disciples were filled with the Holy Spirit at the time of the Feast of Weeks (Pentecost), one hundred and twenty were gathered in the upper room. When Solomon dedicated the first temple in Jerusalem, one hundred and twenty priests sounded the trumpets to give praise and thanks to God and said: "For He is good, for His mercy endures forever" (2 Chronicles 5:12–13), and "...the glory of the Lord filled the house of God" (verse 14), the same as what took place on the day of Pentecost and in the same city, Jerusalem.

On the day of Pentecost, when Peter stood to preach his first sermon, he quoted the prophet Joel regarding what he and the other disciples had just experienced. 'But this is what was spoken by the prophet Joel', "And it shall come to pass in the last days", says God, "that I will pour out my Spirit on all flesh." ' Peter then continued with his quotation from Joel: "I will show wonders in Heaven above and signs in the earth beneath; blood and fire and vapor of smoke. The sun shall be turned into darkness, and the moon into blood, before the coming of the great and awesome day of the Lord" (Acts 2:16–17, 19–20).

Peter, in referring to Joel (Joel lived around 830 B.C.), quoted from Joel's prophecy, which can be found in Joel chapter two. Peter, however, did not quote Joel's prophecy in full, for if he had done so Peter would have informed his listeners that Joel also referred to: "The threshing floors will be full of wheat and the vats shall overflow with new wine and oil" (Joel 2:24).

In a remarkable way Joel's prophecy links Israel's wheat harvest, the Feast of Weeks, with the heavenly harvest, which commenced on the day of Pentecost, with signs in the sun and moon which originated on the fourth day. A few years ago I was enthralled to learn that man's complete DNA is made up of just four compounds.

Since the first week of creation, the basics have never been altered. The events that took place on *Day Four*, the Jewish Feast of Weeks (the *fourth feast*), the promise of Jesus in sending the Holy

Spirit at the time of the Feast of Weeks to prepare God's kingdom for a harvest of souls; each has followed a divine concept that was first revealed in Genesis chapter one and which could only have been fulfilled by Jesus.

Day Five

"Then God said, 'Let the waters abound with an abundance of living creatures, and let birds fly above the earth across the face of the firmament of the heavens.' So God created great sea creatures and every living thing that moves, with which the waters abounded, according to their kind, and every winged bird according to its kind. And God saw that it was good. And God blessed them, saying, 'Be fruitful and multiply, and fill the waters in the seas, and let birds multiply on the earth.' So the evening and the morning were the fifth day" (Genesis 1:20–23).

Five is the number for *GRACE* – God's *Goodness and His Mercy* (Psalm 23:6) – and on *Day Five* God created the birds and the sea creatures. Can you imagine what the world would sound like and look like without them? How quiet our fields and gardens would be, how bland the seas and rivers if they lacked any marine creatures.

The billions of birds with their variegated plumages and their insistence on mating only with their own kind (one of God's ordinances), the vast array of sea creatures that inhabit the world's rivers and oceans, all have brought enjoyment to both God and mankind – and they were created on *Day Five*.

The fifth of the *Feasts of the Lord* is the Feast of Trumpets (the Hebrew name is *Rosh HaShanah*, meaning: *Head of the Year*) and is celebrated in the Hebrew calendar on the first day of the seventh month. (Some have suggested that its purpose is to prepare God's people for the arrival nine days later of the sixth day of remembrance, the most awesome day of all, the Day of Atonement.)

In explaining *Sign Two* I suggested that the Feast of Trumpets corresponds to God's *Goodness and His Mercy* (His *Hesed*). The gospel is *Good News* because it explains God's love and His kindness and was designed to bring hope to a lost and broken world. Can you imagine a world with no hope because there was no lovingkindness?

The apostle Paul refers to the gospel as: "I am not ashamed of the gospel of Christ, for it is the power of God to salvation for everyone who believes, for the Jew first and also the Greek (Gentile)" (Romans 1:16). The gospel is indeed *Good News* for Jew and Gentile alike, for all who believe.

Concerning the *Fifth Day* and the emergence of God's *Grace*, E. W. Bullinger has noted: "Grace means favour; but what kind of favour, for favour is of many kinds. Favour shown to the miserable we call mercy; favour shown to the poor we call pity; favour shown to the obstinate we call patience; but

favour shown to the unworthy we call GRACE!"
Bullinger also points out the five great mysteries of
God, these being:

1. The Father
2. The Son
3. The Spirit
4. Creation
5. Redemption

Redemption (the *Fifth Mystery*) is the act of God's
Grace, and *Grace* was initiated on the *Fifth Day*,
predating man on the *Sixth Day*. Redemption is
what we inherit from the saving work of Jesus, His
Goodness and His *Mercy*, and it can be observed in
Day Five, the Feast of Trumpets – the *Fifth* Feast –
and in Jesus Himself, for He is the fulfilment of
God's goodness and His mercy, God's love and His
kindness. See Isaiah 55:7.

When God blessed the sea creatures and the birds,
He said to them: "Be fruitful and multiply, and fill
the waters in the seas, and let birds multiply on the
earth." That God commanded the sea creatures and
the birds to multiply, to fill the seas and the earth; is
it not a curious thing that God should have told
them to do so, His first command? Not so, and this
is an appropriate time to perhaps consider why.

As with God's command for the sea creatures and
the birds to multiply, to fill the seas and the earth –
it continues to be a mystery that birds are able to fly
thousands of miles and fish to swim thousands of

miles and then to return to where they were born –
the same instruction was given by Jesus to His
disciples to: "Go therefore and make disciples of all
nations, baptizing them in the name of the Father
and of the Son and of the Holy Spirit" (Matthew
28:19). His words are how Jesus reiterated God's
first command to the sea creatures and the birds.

Jesus' command to His disciples as recorded by
Mark is also worth recalling: "Go into all the world
and preach the gospel to every creature. He who
believes and is baptized will be saved; but he who
does not believe will be condemned" (Mark 16: 15–
16).

Finally, the last command of Jesus to His disciples:
"…you shall be witnesses of Me in Jerusalem, and
in Judea and Samaria, and to the end of the earth"
(Acts 1:8).

When God told the fish and birds to multiply, it was
before man was created on the sixth day. God's
command to the fish and the birds is an amazing
precursor of what Jesus was to say to His disciples –
*'to go into the world and multiply, to make other
disciples and to fill the world with My disciples.'*

Today, the command of Jesus has been largely
fulfilled, the gospel has been preached to the ends
of the earth and Jerusalem, which was subjugated
by the nations for nearly two thousand years, has
been returned to the Children of Israel as the times
of the Gentiles draws to a close (Luke 21:24).

Day Six

We have now arrived at the final day in creation's story, *Day Six*. (*Day Seven* was a rest day.) The question therefore is: Does *Day Six* correspond in any way to the Day of Atonement, the sixth period of remembrance, and if so, what are the *Signs*?

"Then God said, 'Let the earth bring forth the living creature according to its kind; cattle and creeping thing and beast of the earth, each according to its kind'; and it was so. And God made the beast of the earth according to its kind, cattle according to its kind, and everything that creeps on the earth according to its kind. And God saw that it was good. Then God said, 'Let Us make man in Our image, according to Our likeness; let them have dominion over the fish of the sea, over the birds of the air (created on Day Five), and over the cattle, over all the earth and over every creeping thing that creeps on the earth.' So God created man in His own image; in the image of God He created Him; male and female He created them" (Genesis 1:24–27).

"Then God saw everything that He had made, and indeed it was very good. So the evening and the morning were the sixth day" (Genesis 1:31).

It is here that the concept of a triumvirate God – "Let 'Us' make man in 'Our' image, according to 'Our' likeness," – is introduced. The concept of God being anything other than *One* is hard for some

112

to accept, particularly for Jewish people for who a monotheistic deity is cardinal to their faith. For example: "Hear O Israel: The Lord our God is one! You shall love the Lord your God with all your heart, with all your soul, and with all your strength" (Deuteronomy 6:4–5). These words are known by Jewish people as *The Shema*.

Although God is described here in Deuteronomy as being *One*, which is correct, it is here that the concept of *three in one* is also given: "your heart, your soul and your strength." There are, of course, other Scriptures where God is portrayed as being a divine entity other than One Person, such as in Psalm 2:7 where God declares: "You are My Son, today I became Your Father." And in Ezekiel, "Thus says the Lord God: 'O house of Israel, let Us have no more of your abominations...'" (Ezekiel 44:6). God's rebuke to His people is in the plural, not the singular. *(Author's underlining)*

On the sixth day, God's instruction to Adam and his wife Eve was that they were to exercise dominion over all the plants and creatures that God had made. "And God said. 'See, I have given you every herb that yields seed which is on the face of all the earth, and every tree whose fruit yields seed; to you it shall be for food. Also, to every beast of the earth, to every bird of the air, and to everything that creeps on the earth, in which there is life, I have given every green herb for food' and it was so" (Genesis 1:29–30). Dominion can also mean authority. Compare God's instruction to Adam and

Eve to what Jesus said to the Jews: "For as the Father has <u>life in Himself</u>, so He has granted the Son to have <u>life in Himself</u>, and has given Him authority to execute judgment also, <u>because He is the Son of Man</u>" (John 5:26–27). *(Author's underlining)*

The fact that man was created on the sixth day and the Day of Atonement is the sixth appointed time in the cycle of seven, indicates that if God wanted to set aside a *Day* as an everlasting memorial for His Son's birth, then these two events must be related. What took place on the sixth day and what took place at the time of the sixth remembrance indicates that God's decision to send Jesus was taken before Genesis was written. The Day of Atonement was God's choice; this Day was planned in advance.

When God decided on a way to renew His relationship with man, but without man's sin, for God is Holy, God knew that the initiative would have to be His. From the fall of man, man's disregard of God, true fellowship with God would again only be possible if God was willing and able to establish a way of restoring man back to Himself, because man who had become sinful was incapable of achieving his own redemption.

God knew that the work of atonement would be costly (it very nearly cost Abraham the life of his son Isaac) so that when God sent His Son it was because Jesus was the only One by which "…we must be saved" (Acts 4:12). Jesus is frequently referred to in the New Testament as being *The Son of God*, but He is also referred to as being *The Son of* Man, a phrase that is a typical Hebraism, meaning: *Partaking of the nature of.*

The apostle Paul in his letter to the Philippians explains this as: "…Christ Jesus, who being in the form of God, did not consider it robbery to be equal with God, but made Himself of no reputation, taking the form of a bondservant, and coming in the likeness of men. And being found in appearance as a man, He humbled Himself and became obedient to the point of death, even the death of the cross" (Philippians 2:6–8). Does this mean that at His birth Jesus became something less than God? No, of course not, "For in Him (Jesus) dwells all the fullness of the Godhead bodily" (Colossians 2:9).

If the biblical description of creation has ever caused you problems, that God made the earth, the sun, the moon and the stars also, and that He created all that was needed for life to exist in just six days (and He then rested on the seventh day), do not be too concerned. God, I am sure, can accept us with our doubts, as Jesus accepted Thomas with his doubts. Personally, I do believe that God created the heavens and the earth; however, I'm not overly concerned about the way He did so, similar to how I'm not too concerned about how computers work.

What is important is the pattern which God established, because the six days, followed by the seventh day for rest, are a description of a cycle of days, seasons and years that was further enhanced

115

in the cycle of the *Seven Feasts of the Lord*. And, within these cycles of time, there exists incredible design which includes *Time* and *Signs* as indicated in Genesis 1:14.

Times and *Signs* are also referred to concerning Jesus, such as His *Hour* that had not yet arrived; or His *Hour* that had arrived. A number of the miracles that Jesus performed are also referred to as being *Signs*. Signs in Scripture are complementary; they help us to understand who God is and who Jesus is and what it was that He came to do for us.

During the many years I have believed in Jesus, I have come to learn that there is a great deal of detail within the Hebrew Scriptures about Jesus' birth, life, death and resurrection, that it's essential I study the Hebrew Scriptures if I want to know more and understand more about Jesus. For example, when we read about Adam in Genesis chapter two, we read that God said: "It is not good that man should be alone; I will make him a helper comparable to him" (Genesis 2:18). Therefore: "...the Lord God caused a deep sleep to fall on Adam, and he slept; and He took one of his ribs, and closed up the flesh in its place. Then the rib which the Lord God had taken from man He made into woman, and He brought her to the man. And Adam said: 'This is now bone of my bones, and flesh of my flesh; she shall be called Woman, because she was taken out of Man'" (Genesis 2:21–23). Is this detail of Eve's creation not a representation of what God did to establish companionship with us when Jesus died, when a Roman soldier took a spear and *pierced the side of Jesus*?

Today, the Church, which is described in the New Testament as being *The Body,* or, *The Bride of Christ* (and which initially was 100 percent Jewish but now includes many Gentiles who have been grafted into God's family), is able to trace its spiritual birth back to when the incision was made in Jesus' side and "… blood and water came out" of the wound (John 19:34).

In Acts 20:28, the apostle Paul refers to "…the church of God which He (Jesus) purchased with his own blood." And, in Paul's letter to the Ephesians, Paul wrote: "…the husband is head of the wife, as also Christ is head of the church; and He is the Saviour of the body" (Ephesians 5:23).

Having looked at the biblical account of creation (Genesis chapter one) and the *Seven Feasts of the Lord* (Leviticus 23), and having seen how these two chapters are intertwined and point us to Jesus, it was then that I began to see God's plan of salvation in much clearer detail following the breakdown of God's original intention (but not through any failing on God's part), which is what happened when Adam and Eve disobeyed God. When they disobeyed, if sin was not to end man's relationship with God forever, then God needed to provide a way to restore man back to Himself. God's plan for the future is what is described in the Hebrew Bible (The Old Testament) and the implementation of

God's plan is what is described in the New Testament, which commenced with the miraculous birth of our Saviour, Jesus. The Day of Atonement, the Sixth appointed time for remembrance, the sixth day, the day when man was created, is surely the most appropriate time for Jesus to have been born?

The Apostle Paul

In Paul's letter to the Colossians, Paul describes God's contingency plan. In the following passage there are several similarities regarding this passage and Scriptures quoted earlier, particularly from Genesis and Leviticus. The similarities are not surprising because Paul understood that God is basically very methodical when it comes to the effectiveness of implementing His perfect plan.

Paul, who gives: "…thanks to the Father who has qualified us to be partakers of the inheritance of the saints in light. He (that is God) has delivered us from the power of darkness and conveyed us into the kingdom of the Son of His love, in whom we have redemption through His blood, the forgiveness of sins. He (that is God's Son, Jesus) is the image of the invisible God, the firstborn over all creation. For by Him all things were created that are in Heaven and that are on the earth, visible and invisible, whether thrones or dominions or principalities or powers. All things were created through Him and for Him. And He is before all things, and in Him all things consist. And He is the head of the body, the church, who is the beginning, the firstborn from the dead, that in all things He may have the preeminence (Colossians 1:12–18).

And Paul also writes: "And so it is written, 'The first man Adam became a living being.' The last Adam became a life giving spirit. However, the spiritual is not the first, but the natural, and afterward the spiritual. The first man was of the earth, made of dust; the second Man is the Lord from Heaven. As was the man of dust, so also are those made of dust; and as the heavenly Man, so also are those who are heavenly. And as we have borne the image of the man of dust, we shall also bear the image of the heavenly Man" (1 Corinthians 15:45–49).

When Jesus died (*the last Adam*), the Church – which in Scripture is described as being *'The Bride of Christ'* – was created, the same as when Eve was created out of the side of her husband Adam. The creation by God of men and women and the birth of Jesus are so intrinsically linked to each other that there has to be a physical and a spiritual connection that ties these two events together.

Is it that man who was made on the *Sixth Day*, and Jesus who was born at the time of the *Sixth Feast* – the Day of Atonement – are so similar, that Jesus' birth must have been planned in advance to enable mankind to be reconciled back to God?

God who chose the day for the Day of Atonement? He and no other?

In Hebrews we read: "You, Lord, in the beginning laid the foundation of the earth, and the heavens are the work of Your hands" (Hebrews 1:10). What took place in the beginning involved God, and also His Son, Jesus. God knew that if man sinned, that He, God, would need to find a way, an effective way, of introducing a method of atonement as a means whereby fellowship between Himself and man could be renewed.

The apostle John refers to the origin of God's plan when he noted that in Heaven there exists: "...the Book of Life of the Lamb <u>slain from the foundation of the world</u>" (Revelation 13:8). *(Author's underlining)* The plan originated in the beginning; Jesus was always going to be the One who would be its focus.

Very nearly, this completes my research into the question I once asked, and more than once: *When was Jesus REALLY born?* There is, of course, one day still to go. What has gone before, God's involvement in creation and the birth and the death of His Son, Jesus, followed by His resurrection and His return to His Father, can now be seen as God's plan for man's destiny. The plan was to establish an opportunity for man to know God and to be able to tabernacle with Him, to enjoy God by being in His presence and to experience His rest, as He Himself "...rested on the seventh day from all His work which He had done (Genesis 2:2).

The cycle, which continues to the present time with its weekly remembrance, is about to be completed.

Day Seven

Today, it appears, man generally has reached the stage where he no longer wants to know God; activity and entertainment seem to be his main objective and the concept and purpose of a weekly day of rest has largely been forgotten. As a result, most seem to be living at a distance from God. However, for those who wish to know God, there exists the opportunity for them to discover God's joy and God's rest. The way to enjoy God's rest is to carefully study and prayerfully seek to understand God's plan. True rest can only be discovered as we follow the detail as found in God's blueprint. This, God has explained, can only be found in His Son, Jesus.

"Thus the heavens and the earth, and all the host of them, were finished. And on the seventh day God ended His work which He had done, and He rested on the seventh day from all His work which He had done. Then God blessed the seventh day and sanctified it, (God made it 'Holy') because in it He rested from all His work which God had created and made" (Genesis 2:1–3).

On *Day Seven* God rested, which brings us to the seventh feast, the Feast of Tabernacles, sometimes referred to as: "…the Feast of Ingathering at the end of the year, when you have gathered in the fruit of your labors from the field" (Exodus 23:16). Seven in Hebrew indicates *Spiritual Perfection* and the seventh feast, the Feast of Tabernacles (or

Ingathering) was designed by God to establish an opportunity for man to rest from his labour at the end of the working year.

Rest is observed by Jewish people when they keep the Feast of Tabernacles, when all their work in providing food for themselves has ended, and it is what we, too, may experience in the perfect rest that Jesus has provided for those who believe in Him.

The experience is known as being in *His Rest* and virtually all of Hebrews chapter four is given over to describing this concept of an eternal rest. The Feast of Tabernacles (when the final harvest is gathered in) is not the only occasion when God's people may benefit by resting. There is also the *Seventh Day* of rest from man's labor, the Sabbath.

In Exodus there is an intriguing account about Moses when he left the camp of the Children of Israel and took his tent with him. Far from the camp, Moses pitched his tent and called it: "...the tabernacle of meeting." There, at his tent, "...the Lord spoke to Moses face to face, as a man speaks to his friend." God said to Moses: "I know you by name, and you have also found grace in My sight." Having been reassured, Moses prayed, and then God said to him: "My presence will go with you, and I will give you rest" (Exodus 33:7–14). *(Author's underling)* For those who consider themselves as being God's people, God's children, should they not also experience God's rest as they learn what it is to tabernacle with God?

Jesus said: "Come to Me, all you who labor and are heavy laden, and I will give you rest. Take my yoke upon you and learn from Me, for I am gentle and lowly in heart and you will find rest for your souls" (Matthew 11: 28–29).

Concerning the keeping of the Feast of Tabernacles, the Lord spoke to Moses, saying: "Speak to the children of Israel, saying: The fifteenth day of this seventh month shall be the Feast of Tabernacles for seven days to the Lord. On the first day there shall be a holy convocation. You shall do no customary work on it. For seven days you shall offer an offering made by fire to the Lord. On the eighth day you shall have a holy convocation, and you shall offer an offering made by fire to the Lord. It is a sacred assembly, and you shall do no customary work on it" (Leviticus 23:33–36).

The Feast of Tabernacles, the seventh feast, is a time for rest and is to be observed for seven days during the seventh month of the Hebrew calendar. When Jesus went up to Jerusalem to attend the Feast of Tabernacles, it was on the last day of the feast that He stood and said aloud: "If anyone thirsts, let him come to Me and drink. He who believes in Me, as the Scripture has said, out of his heart will flow rivers of living water" (John 7:37–38).

Tom Wright in his study of John's gospel, *John for Everyone*, comments on this passage: "Among the prayers that were regularly prayed at the festival were prayers for rain and for the resurrection of the dead; so not only the theme of water, but also of new life, were spot on subjects that would be in people's minds."

Only a few hours before He was crucified, and in a way that He had not done so previously, Jesus said to His disciples: "Let not your heart be troubled; you believe in God, believe also in Me. In my Father's house are many mansions; if it were not so, I would have told you. I go to prepare a place for you. And if I go and prepare a place for you, I will come again and receive you to Myself; that where I am, there you may be also" (John 14:1–3).

The temporary shelter used by Jewish people during the Feast of Tabernacles – *The Sukkot* – is to be superseded by a resting place that Jesus is preparing for those who love Him and are eagerly awaiting His calling, that together the two might experience rest.

Jesus' rest is symbolized in God's day of rest, which God and creation observed on the day after Adam was created. Later, it was replicated in the Feast of Tabernacles, the seventh observance that follows five days after the Day of Atonement. Five is a *Sign* of grace.

"For since the creation of the world God's invisible attributes are clearly seen, being understood by the things that are made, even His eternal power and Godhead…" (Romans 1:20).

PATTERNS AND PATENTS

Following the Exodus of the Children of Israel from Egypt, they then journeyed east to Mount Sinai, the Mountain of God, and it was here that God told Moses to construct the Tabernacle for God to dwell in, in the midst of His people. Conversely, the Tabernacle also enabled the Children of Israel to draw near to God.

Moses was commanded to make the Tabernacle according to a pattern that God had revealed to Moses. "And let them make Me a sanctuary, that I may dwell among them. According to all that I show you, that is, the pattern of the tabernacle and the pattern of all its furnishings, just so shall you make it" (Exodus 25:8–9).

When it came to designing the Tabernacle, God was not only the architect, He was also the patent owner; therefore, Moses, God's servant, made the Tabernacle according to what God had shown him.

Abraham's response was similar. "By faith Abraham obeyed when he was called to go out to the place which he would receive as an inheritance. And he went out, not knowing where he was going. By faith he dwelt in the land of promise as in a foreign country, dwelling in tents with Isaac and Jacob, the heirs with him of the same promise; for he waited for the city which has foundations, whose builder and maker is God" (Hebrews 11:8–10).

God promised Abraham and His descendants a dwelling place. "Therefore God is not ashamed to be called their God, for He has prepared a city for them" (Hebrews 11:16).

God's patterns and His patents have been in existence from the time of Genesis. "All Scripture is given by inspiration of God…" (2 Timothy 3:16), therefore, it is not surprising that we should see God's plans and His purposes as transcribed in His Holy Word.

Robin and A. Wiseman

Earlier I recalled my visit to Israel in February 2013 and it was in Tel Aviv that I met a South African medical scientist who does not believe in time.

Robin, who is Jewish, told me that he sees time as being an invention of man, and man, Robin said, "…has become a slave to time." Four months earlier, Robin informed me, he had been robbed at gunpoint and his watch had been stolen. When I met Robin his arm was still bare; Robin had not replaced his watch!

Robin also confessed that he does not believe in God. Not only had Robin lost his appreciation of the importance of time, Robin had also lost his ancestral belief in God.

In the way that man today uses time, I can agree with Robin, but it's not time that is at fault. That time exists in creation, sequence, patterns and beauty, in order to show the nature, order, power and wonder of God, is simply breath taking.

The day after I met Robin, I then met Dr. Allen Wiseman, Ph.D., a Canadian born Jew and holder of a doctorate in Jewish philosophy. My meetings with Robin and with Dr. Wiseman were not planned, but the two encounters had a resonance of having been planned, for they took place on successive days and in the same restaurant – one person from South Africa, the next from Canada, and myself from England.

After the first rather negative discussion about time with Robin, the following day in conversation with Dr. Wiseman I explained to him briefly how I came to believe that Jesus was born on the Day of Atonement.

Dr. Wiseman also believes in Jesus, and as I explained the *Fifth Sign* for Jesus' birth, based on my recent discovery that Genesis chapter one and Leviticus chapter twenty-three appear to be reciprocal, Dr. Wiseman informed me that he had recently written a pamphlet about these same chapters, having arrived at the same conclusion!

To have met a gifted academic (in Israel) within two weeks of being inspired to observe a connection between the Genesis account of creation and the *Seven Feasts of the Lord*, was extraordinary, particularly with someone with the initial and surname *A. Wiseman*! As promised, a few days later, Dr. Wiseman forwarded to me details of his

DAVID HAMSHIRE

own conclusions. With Dr. Wiseman's permission,
I would like to quote part of what he has written
concerning the link between the *Seven Days* of
creation and the *Seven Feasts of the Lord.*

> *"Seven holy appointed times or feasts mark
> the yearly, Biblical calendar. God initiated
> the series in Exodus 12, to be fully listed in
> Leviticus 23. These times represent a pattern
> of scripture that begins with the seven days or
> periods of creation week that are echoed by
> the regular weekly cycle, and further
> elaborated in Israel's deliverance from
> Egyptian slavery. Just as creation continues
> until the end of time, so to do the effects of
> these seven feasts. Both the repetition of the
> weekly cycle and the seven yearly holidays
> remind us of real past events that also point to
> the prophetic future. As such, these feasts are
> more than ordinary holidays. While the
> regular weekly and yearly cycles ingrain in us
> a down-to-earth rhythm in life, the linear
> process gives us an overall perspective that
> spans from the very beginning of creation to
> the ultimate completion of God's redemptive
> purposes.*

> *"Historically, because the Christian world
> veered away from its Jewish roots in the early
> centuries, the larger scope and significance of*

> *the Lord's seven feasts (aside from Passover) were often overlooked, or not sufficiently understood."*

Having noted only two weeks previously the similarity of Genesis chapter one and Leviticus chapter twenty three, my unexpected meeting with Dr. A. Wiseman was simply the icing on the cake.

Regarding design in creation, which is so dependent on the seasonal cycle of *time*, design is a parameter; it determines the framework for the existence and the continuation of life; be it plant, animal, or human. Regarding Jesus, His birth was according to a pattern designed and patented by God. Bethlehem was where He was to be born and Calvary, on the outskirts of Jerusalem, was where He was to die, thirty-three and a half years later. Understandably, because of the foreknowledge of God, the planning was carried out long before each event took place and the detail of each event can be found in the Bible's prophecies concerning Jesus.

Jesus' journey through life, much like our own journey, can be described as: *"all the days of His life."* Jesus was born to become a High Priest; it was His destiny (Hebrews 9:11). In *Sign Five*, once I had embarked on following Jesus in Genesis and had seen creation as being in tandem with the *Seven Feasts of the Lord* – confirmed as explained in *Sign Two* by Psalm 23 – what was especially riveting was to see how Jesus is portrayed in an identical sequence, culminating in His final dwelling place,

His own *Sabbath*, His own time of rest. To have seen how Jesus is portrayed in creation has been a remarkable revelation; it is now so clear, so obvious, but why did I not understand these things before? Perhaps, because, they had never been explained to me before?

To summarize God's intention for Jesus, for the Scriptures (*The Sacred Writings*) as He Himself said: "…these are they which testify of Me" (John 5:39), the most appropriate time to begin is to begin at the beginning, *Day One.*

- Day One. Jesus, the *Light of the World*, *Cut Off* (extinguished) at Passover, the first observance, is the One who sets us free from sin. "If the Son makes you free, you shall be free indeed" (John 8:36).
- Day Two. Jesus, in whose name we are baptized in the parting of the waters, has provided the gift of His righteousness to separate us from our unrighteousness, as remembered in the Feast of Unleavened Bread, the second observance, enabling His followers to enter the Kingdom of Heaven (the Promised Land being God's destiny for His people after their deliverance from slavery in Egypt).
- Day Three. Jesus' resurrection from the confinement of the earth after three days, as observed in the Feast of Firstfruits, the third

observance, for Jesus to become the first of the Firstfruits of those who will rise again from the earth; from death.

- Day Four. Jesus' work while it was still day, so celebrating the harvest of the Feast of Weeks, the fourth observance, and His promise of the gift of the Holy Spirit to be used for God's redemptive purposes in order to create a harvest of souls in the world that God has made.

- Day Five. Jesus' command to His disciples to *'go into all the world'* to proclaim God's *Goodness* and His *Mercy*, the gospel as remembered in the Feast of Trumpets, the fifth observance, recalling God's earlier command to the birds and the fish to fill the earth and the seas with their kind.

- Day Six. Jesus, the *Son of God*, became the *Son of Man*, encapsulating in the purposeful timing of His birth, His own Day of Atonement experience, the sixth observance, that we might enter into God's presence beyond the Veil.

- Day Seven. Jesus' provision of rest, that all believers might be able to Tabernacle with Him, the seventh observance, because He has gone to prepare a resting place for those who respect, trust and obey God.

In *Sign One* I referred to numbers in Hebrew thought and explained how the numbers seven and ten are associated with the Day of Atonement – the tenth day of the seventh month. In *Sign Five* and also in this subsection, I have continued by referring to the *Seven Days of Creation* and the *Seven Feasts of the Lord* by explaining how the two are interwoven, like a tapestry designed to enthrall as a result of its designer's intricate attention to detail.

In an article in the *British Church Newspaper* (July 13th, 2012), John Willans, B.D., under the headline *"The Mathematical Patterns of Scripture"* wrote how seven in Scripture appears not as a coincidence but as evidence of a divine plan. In his assessment of the way seven is portrayed in Scripture, Willans concluded: "This sevenfold structure is found throughout Scripture and is unique to the Bible. The number seven underlies and permeates the text in every way possible. These patterns aren't found in any other ancient literature and the examples never seem to come to an end. This sevenfold pattern in Scripture interlocks paragraph with paragraph and book with book."

Willans also explained how the genealogy of Jesus and His birth illustrates how Jesus was intrinsically linked to the number seven. Seven is also linked to the opening statement in Genesis, for in Hebrew the introduction uses just seven words.

When God created the earth, He also made man with the intention for man to: "…do justly, love mercy, and walk humbly with God" (Micah 6:8).

Sadly, because of the "lust of the flesh, the lust of the eyes, and the pride of life, which is not of the Father but is of this world" (1John 2:16), God's intention for mankind became void, but not forever, for God had in reserve a plan that would involve Himself, the Holy Spirit, and His Son, Jesus. But for God's plan to succeed, it would need:

- God's willingness to implement His plan.
- The involvement of the Holy Spirit (that Mary might become pregnant).
- The agreement and commitment of the only One who could make the plan operative, Jesus. For Jesus, it would mean His birth, to be followed by His death, even though He never sinned.

The Jewish Day of Atonement and the Passover observance are the only two times that appear as being suitable for Jesus' birth and His death. If not the Day of Atonement, when? If not the Day of Atonement, why did God choose this day from all the other days available to Him for the Children of Israel to observe God's patterns and His patents?

To Job, God asked: "Where were you when I laid the foundations of the earth? Tell Me, if you have understanding. Who determined its measurements? Surely you know!" " Can you bind the cluster of the Pleiades (the Seven Stars), or loose the belt of Orion? Can you bring out Mazzaroth in its season? (Constellations). Or can you guide the Great Bear with its cubs? Do you know the ordinances of the heavens? Can you set their dominion over the earth?" (Job 38:4–5, 31–33). The psalmist also took note of God taking the initiative. "O Lord, how manifold are Your works! In wisdom you have made them all. The earth is full of Your possessions…" (Psalm 104:24).

God's decision to send Jesus would have been extremely hard, but "…God so loved the world" (John 3:16). God knew that Jesus would have to die and then rise again, "…according to the Scriptures" (1 Corinthians 15:3–4). It was a sacrifice that God knew would one day take place, but it was one that God was prepared for, for He was willing to give up His only Son. For those who believe in Jesus and have entrusted their lives to Him, the words of Paul to the Corinthians are sufficient to enable all to know that God's plans and His purposes have been perfected in the person of His Son, Jesus.

"But now is Christ risen from the dead, and has become the firstfruits of those who have fallen asleep. For since by man (Adam) came death, by Man (Jesus) also came the resurrection of the dead. For as in Adam all die, even so in Christ shall all be made alive. But each one in his own order: Christ the firstfruits, afterward those who are Christ's at His coming. Then comes the end, when He delivers the kingdom to God the Father, when He puts an end to all rule and all authority and power. For He must reign till He has put all enemies under His feet. The last enemy that will be destroyed is death. For 'He has put all things under His feet.' …that God may be all in all" (1 Corinthians 15:20–28).

WHAT'S IN A NAME?

In describing the *Five Signs*, what I have tried to do is to provide a basic insight into the framework of God's plan in sending Jesus, and why His birth-day was (and is) so significant. Other *Signs* concerning His birth almost certainly do exist, and at the end of this section I have provided a possible *Sixth Sign* – What's in a Name? The *Five Signs* for Jesus' birth on the Day of Atonement are as follows:

1. God's attention to detail – the allocation of *Time*.
2. God's appointed observances – the *Seven Feasts*.
3. God's revealing Word – the *Bible*.
4. God's appointed representative – His *High Priest*.
5. God's creative works – what God made and described as being *'Good'*, or *'Very Good'*.

What previously I had not understood was the link which connects the timing for Jesus' birth, the Day of Atonement, to God's plan of salvation. Genesis records the work of creation which, when complete, *"...on the seventh day God ended His work which He had done, and He rested on the seventh day from all His work which He had done."* (Genesis 2:2). God's creative works were later recalled in the *Seven Feasts of the Lord*, but their fulfilment would not be complete until Jesus came, who explained: *"...for the works which the Father has given Me to finish – the very works that I do – bear witness of Me, that the Father has sent Me."* (John 5:36). A little later, Jesus prayed to His Father and said: *"I have glorified You on the earth. I have finished the work which You have given Me to do."* (John17:4). *(Author's underlining)* The following day, when He was suspended between earth and Heaven, Jesus said: "It is finished" (John 19:30). Finally, His work on earth was complete.

Now in His Father's presence, Jesus' destiny was for Him to work for and represent others. This is the value of knowing why in the life of Jesus the Day of Atonement is so significant; that at His birth He came from God to bring us into union with God, and that at Passover, when His work was complete, He was able to return to the Father to represent us as our Saviour and our Mediator.

Could I be wrong in saying that Jesus was born on the Day of Atonement? Yes, of course I could. Does God exist? I believe so, but not everyone believes in God. Eternity will confirm if I have understood correctly God's Word, but I am convinced of when Jesus was born because it was to the Bible that I turned for my evidence.

In making my research known, it was never my intention to provide a detailed description about what Jewish people do on the Day of Atonement, apart from the fact that it is day of prayer and fasting. For an understanding of the importance of this Day, passages such as Leviticus chapters sixteen and twenty three, Psalm twenty three and the book of Hebrews, provide volumes of detail for those willing to spend time in carrying out their own study. Also, today, most have access to the internet and any search facility will be able to list numerous web sites where additional information can be sourced. When it comes to books about the *Seven Feasts of the Lord*, once again there is an endless supply of good material readily available.

The Day of Atonement is both historically and currently a most *Awesome Day* and is as equally important as the day when Jesus died on the eve of Passover. My objective in producing this book has been that believers, Jew and Gentile alike, might comprehend what the Day of Atonement teaches us about Jesus. The relevance and its benefit is that we might understand Jesus and God's plan of salvation in ways we may not have considered previously.

In the past an element of confusion may have existed in that Hellenism, a Greek presentation of Christianity, has tended to dominate our understanding of Jesus, rather than understanding Him in His Jewish context and in the Hebrew Bible's (the Old Testament) presentation of Him. The practice of observing the *Seven Feasts of the Lord* is to help believers understand Jesus, in particular His appointment as a Saviour, and is one of the most basic lessons to be understood when a person becomes a believer in Jesus. Recalling His birth on the Day of Atonement seems to me to make more sense than setting aside another day, a non-Biblical day, for the remembrance of His birth.

In the book of Exodus are recorded the details of a meeting which God had with Moses; it was when God made Himself known to Moses at a burning bush. When God called to Moses, Moses replied: *"Here I am."* When God told Moses what He wanted him to do, Moses said: *"Who am I..."* When Moses asked God what His name was, God replied: *"I AM WHO I AM"* and God said: *"Thus you shall say to the children of Israel, I AM has sent me to you."* (Exodus 3:2–14).

At the time of the Day of Atonement observance, for Jewish people there is always an emphasis on repentance to enable the penitent to bond with God in commitment and companionship. In his burning bush experience, God instructed Moses: "Do not draw near this place. Take your sandals off your feet, for the place where you stand is holy ground" (Exodus 3:5). Jewish tradition requires that when observing the Day of Atonement, leather shoes should not be worn, because, like Moses at the burning bush, for those recalling this remembrance, God is a holy God.

Such an experience has been aptly commented upon by Elizabeth Browning:

> *"Earth's crammed with Heaven,*
> *and every common bush afire with God;*
> *but only he who sees takes off his shoes."*

When Jesus was asked: "Who do You make yourself out to be?" He replied: "Most assuredly, I say to you, before Abraham was, I AM" (John 8:53 & 57). The eternal heart-cry of God can be summarized in just nine words: "I am your God and you are My people", words which are repeated frequently throughout the Hebrew Bible and the New Testament. Herein is the assurance that God wishes to establish a relationship between Himself and His people, but it can only happen through Jesus. For such a relationship to exist, it is necessary to know God's gift of *Atonement*, for without Jesus there is no hope whatsoever of knowing who God is.

While the confirmation of Jesus' birth, His ministry, death and resurrection are provided in the New Testament, the prophetic promises, including the when and the where and the spiritual relevance of each event, are first recorded in the Hebrew Bible, written many years before Jesus' birth. This is perhaps why Jesus in helping two of His disciples to understand what had recently taken place in Jerusalem, referred to: "... Moses and all the Prophets" and He then "...expounded to them in all the Scriptures the things concerning Himself" (Luke 24:27). At the time when this meeting between Jesus and two of His disciples took place, there was no New Testament. Jesus, however, was not limited in enabling His disciples to understand who He was, or what it was that He came to do, because Jesus can so easily be identified in the first section of our Bibles, what Jewish people refer to as the

139

Hebrew Bible – the *Tanakh* – and what Christians refer to as the Old Testament, and it is from these pages in God's Word that I have come to see (I believe) when Jesus was born.

One of my tasks has been to explain how Jesus has fulfilled the *Seven Feasts of the Lord* (or *'Times of Remembrance'*) from Passover through to the Feast of Tabernacles. The order, as transcribed in Leviticus 23 and paraphrased in Psalm 23 (but first made known in Genesis chapter one), follows the Hebrew Religious Calendar. Its sequence commences with the death of Jesus at Passover, which for some may seem a little strange; why does the sequence commence with Jesus' death? One possible answer is that what Jesus came to do was to reverse the process which began when man first sinned and that because of his sin, death became man's consequence.

What happens if we observe the Hebrew Civil Calendar (beginning with the month of Tishrei) and view Jesus' life from when He was born? In setting out such a proposition, I do so on the basis that:

- The seventh month of the Religious Calendar (Tishrei) now becomes the first month of the Civil Calendar.
- The Month Nisan – the first month of the Religious Calendar – now becomes the seventh month of the Civil Calendar – *Seven* being a *Sign* of *Spiritual Perfection*.

When Jesus was born (The Day of Atonement), He came from the real Holy of Holies in Heaven (the one in the Tabernacle was a copy) to become God's High Priest, God's representative, to carry out the Day of Atonement observance Himself; and on the correct day. Jesus then dwelt (Feast of Tabernacles) with those of His generation in order to explain God's plan of salvation to His followers, those He had chosen. "You did not choose Me, but I chose you and appointed you that you should go and bear fruit and that your fruit should remain…" (John 15:16). Then when Jesus died (Passover), because He was righteous (Unleavened Bread), He became God's punishment for man's sin. Pilate said of Him not once, but three times: "I find no fault in Him", yet He was destined to die for the wrongdoing of others.

Three days after His death, on the first day of the week, Jesus was raised from the dead (Firstfruits) because death could not keep Him for He had: "…abolished death and brought life and immortality to light through the Gospel" (2 Timothy 1:10). The resurrection of Jesus would have taken place on the seventeenth day of Nissan, three days and three nights after He was crucified on the fourteenth.

After a waiting period of seven weeks, plus one day – Leviticus 23:16 – Jesus sent the Holy Spirit (Feast of Weeks) to equip with spiritual understanding and power His disciples, whom He had commissioned to preach the Good News of the Gospel. The Gospel is Good News because its message is to proclaim God's Goodness and His Mercy (Feast of Trumpets), His love and His kindness. (Psalm 23:6 & Titus 3:4). As we believe and put our trust in Jesus, we do so knowing that He has promised us the gift of eternal life – (Forever). Jesus speaking: "And this is eternal life, that they may know You, the only true God, and Jesus Christ whom You have sent." (John 17:3).

From whichever direction we may view the life of Jesus (birth to death or death to birth) and seek to understand the times previously appointed by God for Him, the result will always be a portrait of God's goodness and His mercy. When taking note of the portrayal of Jesus as described in God's *Signs of Remembrance*, it is but a glimpse of what has been revealed so that we might begin to know God and how we should respond to Him.

The Hebrew Bible refers to numerous portraits of Jesus, including remarkable similarities with the life of Joseph and in prophecies which populate many of the Psalms and books of the Prophets. However, one of the most descriptive portraits is to be seen in the Tabernacle which became God's dwelling place in the midst of His people, the Children of Israel.

Bezalel, and the meaning of his name

Included in God's detailed instructions about how the Tabernacle was to be constructed, God also identified the one who He had previously chosen to carry out the work. "Then the Lord spoke to Moses, saying: 'See, I have called by name Bezalel the son of Uri, the son of Hur, of the tribe of Judah. And I have filled him with the Spirit of God in wisdom, in understanding, in knowledge, and in all manner of workmanship' " (Exodus 31:1–3). Although others would have assisted Bezalel in helping him to construct the Tabernacle, Bezalel completed one particular task himself. Using his carpentry skills, Bezalel "…made the ark of acacia wood" (Genesis 37:1) which, when completed, was placed in the Holy of Holies for use on the Day of Atonement.

When Mary (maybe Joseph?) placed Jesus in a manger (which was probably of a similar shape and size to the 'Ark of Acacia Wood') could the manger not be seen in sharp relief as being a mirror image of the 'Ark', for this appears to have been the manger's function? Yes, a more appropriate resting place for Jesus would have been for Mary and Joseph to use the Ark of the Covenant in the Holy of Holies as a cradle, because everything about it, its size and shape, its material, its contents (Hebrews 9:4), its location, and the cherubim who spread their wings to cover the Mercy Seat as they faced each other with their faces toward the Mercy Seat, was symbolic of the whole host of heaven when they responded to the birth of Jesus in Bethlehem. The provision of the Ark of the Covenant and its purpose looked forward to Jesus and His coming into the world. However, according to Jewish tradition, during the Second Temple era, there was no longer an Ark in the Temple's Holy of Holies and so an alternative to the

Ark had to be provided. The manger and what it conveyed in its meaning as those from heaven looked down upon the One born to become God's provision of mercy, was a fitting and a humble replacement for the Ark of the Covenant.

Consider now Joseph who was betrothed to Mary, who cared for Mary and her new-born Son, God's Son, the Son of Man. Joseph, like God's servant Bezalel – the name Bezalel in Hebrew means: *'In the shadow of God'* – God appointed both Bezalel and Joseph to become involved in His eternal plan; and was it because:

- Bezalel and Joseph were both carpenters.
- Bezalel and Joseph were both from the tribe of Judah.
- At His birth, Jesus' rightful place was that He should have been in the Holy of Holies on the Day of Atonement, the place where Bezalel's work was located, but instead God chose a more humble location for the time and place for Jesus' birth, the Son of God who also became the Son of Man.
- And Joseph, having been appointed to act as Jesus' foster father, was also acting like Bezalel before him, *'In the shadow of God'*.

When Moses set up the Tabernacle for the first time, Moses "…took the Testimony…" (the two tablets of stone on which God had written the Ten Commandments, Exodus 34:28) "…and put it into the ark." (Exodus 40:20). "Then the cloud covered the tabernacle of meeting, and the glory of the Lord filled the tabernacle. And Moses was not able to enter the tabernacle of meeting, because the cloud rested above it, and the glory of the Lord filled the tabernacle" (Exodus 40:34–35).

The cloud which stood above the Tabernacle and the Ark of the Covenant which Bezalel made in which Moses placed the word of God, written by the hand of God, was but a shadow of what would take place centuries later, when a star appeared to guide the wise men to Bethlehem, which "…went before them, till it came and stood over where the young Child was" (Matthew 2:9). By the light of a star, typified in the cloud by day and the fire by night which appeared over the Tabernacle in the time of Moses, the wise men came to Jesus who Mary had given birth to and who she then placed in a manger. The apostle John describes Jesus as being: "…the Word, and the Word was with God and the Word was God." (John 1:1). Jesus was, is, and will always be, God's testimony, proof that God so loved the world and that we should also love Him; and Jesus, who came willingly to become God's atonement sacrifice.

Could God's choice of Bezalel and what his name and his work represents – like Joseph who acted as Jesus' foster father, *'In the shadow of God'* – be a *Sixth Sign* for Jesus' birth? I believe so, because Bezalel was singularly involved in the making of the Ark of the Covenant and the High Priest's white linen vestments (remember the swaddling cloths

145

which Mary wrapped Jesus in? – Luke 2:7), both of which were to feature so graphically on the Day of Atonement when Divine service was performed by just one appointed individual, Israel's High Priest.

What then of Jesus? "Therefore, holy brethren, partakers of the heavenly calling, consider the Apostle and High Priest of our confession, Christ Jesus, who was faithful to Him who appointed Him, as Moses also was faithful in all his house. For this One has been counted worthy of more glory than Moses, inasmuch as He who built the house has more glory than the house. For every house is built by someone, but He who built all things is God" (Hebrews 3:1–4).

Concerning the Lord Jesus we can never know too much about Him, but we can know so little.

For Jewish believers His name is Yeshua.

For Gentile believers His Name is Jesus.

~ ~ ~

Thank you God for sending Jesus,
Thank you Jesus that you came,
Holy Spirit won't You tell me,
More about His lovely Name.

A PRAYER

Father, please give me eyes to see and ears to hear that I may know Jesus as my Passover redeemer and be welcomed into your presence because of His righteousness. Thank you Father that Jesus was the Firstfruits of those who will rise from the dead and that because of Him, I may live forever.

Father, please help me never to fear death because I am trusting in Jesus; knowing that He has "…abolished death and brought life and immortality to light through the Gospel."

I understand Lord Jesus that you fulfilled the Jewish festival of the Feast of Weeks and I thank you for the gift of the Holy Spirit. Please help me to experience the infilling of your Holy Spirit so that I may bear fruit in your harvest field.

Thank you Father for the Good News of your goodness and your mercy. Help me to remember your love and your kindness which I can experience through knowing Jesus, and to listen to your voice, guiding me.

Lord Jesus, I believe you were born to die to become my Atonement sacrifice and that you are now my High Priest, being in the presence of your Father and remembering me, that I may abide – Tabernacle – in your presence forever.

PSALM 50

In considering and completing the descriptions for the *Five Signs*, naturally I continued to wonder if there was further information to be seen in Scripture about the timing for Jesus' birth, such as Bezalel, and the meaning of his name. Of course I now knew the basics, and I have attempted in the pages of this book to explain my understanding of the significance of Jesus' birth when linked to the Day of Atonement. There is nothing like Scripture to explain Scripture in order to understand Jesus. But, for now, to bring my thoughts to a close, I would like to recall Psalm 50.

My reason for choosing this Psalm is not because I knew it well; that was not so. The reason I have chosen this Psalm is because after I had finished writing up the detail for the *Five Signs*, I experienced a very vivid dream and in the dream I was asked to read Psalm fifty. The following morning I did as I was asked. Included in this Psalm are a number of references to some of the detail included in the *Five Signs*. For example:

- *The Mighty One, God the Lord, has spoken; and called the Earth and the Sun.*
- *From the rising of the Sun to its going down.*
- *God will shine forth in Zion.*
- *God will not keep silent.*
- *His calling is from the Heaven,*
- *To the earth, that He may judge His people.*

- *God's righteousness.*
- *The sacrifice of bulls and goats – the Day of Atonement sacrifice.*
- *The cattle and the birds are His.*
- *The World is His.*
- *Words of warning for the unrighteous.*
- *And, whoever offers praise, let his conduct be right.*

Psalm 50

"The Mighty One, God the Lord, has spoken and called the earth. From the rising of the sun to its going down. Out of Zion, the perfection of beauty, God will shine forth. Our God shall come, and shall not keep silent; a fire shall devour before Him, and it shall be very tempestuous all around Him. He shall call to the heavens from above, and to the earth, that He may judge His people. 'Gather My saints together to Me, those who have made a covenant with Me by sacrifice.' Let the heavens declare His righteousness, for God Himself is judge. Hear, O My people, and I will speak, O Israel, and I will testify against you: I am God, your God! I will not rebuke you for your sacrifices or your burnt offerings, which are continually before Me. I will not take a bull from your house, nor goats out of your folds. For every beast of the forest is Mine, and the cattle on a thousand hills. I know all the birds of the mountains, and the wild beasts of the field are Mine. If I were hungry, I would not tell

149

you; for the world is Mine, and all its fullness. Will I eat the flesh of bulls, or drink the blood of goats? Offer to God thanksgiving, and pay your vows to the Most High. Call upon Me in the day of trouble; I will deliver you, and you shall glorify Me.'

"But to the wicked God says: 'What right do you have to declare My statutes, or take my covenant in your mouth. Seeing you hate instruction and cast My words behind you? When you saw a thief, you consented with him, and have been a partaker with adulterers. You give your mouth to evil, and your tongue frames deceit. You sit and speak against your brother; you slander your own mother's son. These things you have done, and I kept silent; you thought that I was altogether like you; but I will rebuke you, and set them in order before your eyes. Now consider this, you who forget God, lest I tear you in pieces, and there be none to deliver.'

"'Whoever offers praise glorifies Me; and to him who orders his <u>conduct aright</u>, I will show the salvation of God.'" *(Author's underlining)*

God is God and He has no equal, other than to say He is *Three in One*, namely: God the Father, God the Son, and God the Holy Spirit. And each of us have three weaknesses which were first seen in Adam and Eve, namely: *Pride, Disobedience*, and *Lack of Respect* for who God is.

So when it comes to living our lives, there are just three essentials in our conduct we should remember.

Humility. In our conduct, the need to be humble.

"…to everyone who is among you, not to think of himself more highly than he ought to think, but to think soberly, as God has dealt to each a measure of faith" (Romans 12:3).

Integrity. In our conduct, the need to be blameless.

"…that you may become blameless and harmless, children of God without fault in the midst of a crooked and perverse generation, among whom you shine as lights in the world" (Philippians 2:15).

Holiness.   In our conduct, the need to be holy.

"And the Lord spoke, saying: 'You shall be holy, for I the Lord your God am holy'" (Leviticus 19:1–2).

Jesus is the One who has enabled us to be in union with God and He has done so by voluntarily becoming God's gift of atonement, to redeem us back to God.   Of course, Passover is important, because it was when Jesus died to forgive us our sin. But for us to enter the Holy of Holies, into His presence, then our need is for Jesus to be acting as God's High Priest who is now in Heaven interceding on our behalf.

The appointment for Jesus to become God's High Priest is His, from the very beginning, but before

He could do so, first He had to enter this world, and I believe He did so on Yom Kippur, the Day of Atonement. If this was not the allocated day for His birth, then what was the Day of Atonement for; *why was it Set Aside, Sanctified by God, made HOLY?* I can think of no other explanation other than the one that I have provided.

This, surely, must be the day, a most *Awesome Day*, the day when Jesus was REALLY born.

BONUS CONTENT

Thank you for purchasing this valuable book. We trust that it has been a blessing to you in your relationship with Jesus the Messiah.

To say "Thank You" for adding this book to your collection, we want to offer you a FREE GIFT to add to your enjoyment of this important subject.

We have recorded an audio interview with David Hamshire, where he discusses the book and shares in-depth commentary on the birth of Jesus.

You are going to thoroughly enjoy hearing from the author himself as he draws on years of bible study, research and godly wisdom, to share with you insights firmly based on Scripture.

For a FREE downloadable copy of this intriguing interview, please visit the webpage below and request your copy:

www.PerissosGroup.com/bonus225

Again, thank you for becoming our valued reader and customer, and we look forward to serving you in the future.

~ *The Staff at Perissos Media*

HOW TO SHARE THIS BOOK WITH OTHERS

If you have enjoyed and been helped by reading *When Was Jesus REALLY Born* and you would like to share a FREE SAMPLE of the book with friends, family or colleagues, please direct them to any of the following webpages:

www.WhenWasJesusBorn.net/sample

www.PerissosGroup.com/sample225

www.info321.com/sample225

Please feel free to send those links via email, text, social media, or any other means possible, so that the wealth of wisdom in this book can be a blessing to as many people as possible.

The sample is absolutely FREE, and it is delivered in digital, downloadable format for immediate delivery, anywhere in the world.

Share it with them TODAY!

ABOUT THE AUTHOR

My own birth-day took place in December 1943, which means that by the end of 2013 I will have reached my three-score years and ten. What has been significant is that for the majority of those years I have believed in God and in His Son Jesus.

My introduction to who God is happened as a result of my elder brother's miraculous healing from Polio. When Ronald was very near to death's door, our neighbours prayed and Ronald was healed, almost instantly. God, therefore, became very relevant and over the next few years each member of my family dedicated our lives to Him, in love and gratitude.

My sister Clemaine had a particularly close relationship with Jesus, but then suddenly she died as a result of a drowning accident. At the time of the accident, Clemaine was fifteen years old; I was just thirteen.

When I reached the age of fifteen, I knew what I wanted to do – I wanted to work with airplanes. Six months later I joined the Royal Air Force to train as an aircraft electrician. Initially, as I moved from adolescence to manhood, my Christian faith was my rock. Manhood, however, can have its problems, and it was only a matter of time before other attractions began to divert me away from God. Thankfully, the distractions failed to rob me of my faith and the Holy Spirit needed only seven words (first spoken by John the Baptist) to bring me back to Jesus: *"He must increase and I must decrease."* Those seven words changed my life.

Fifteen years in the Royal Air Force was followed by ten years with Rank Xerox as a photocopy service engineer.

Photo-copiers gave way to seven years with Open Doors with Brother Andrew, then fourteen years in financial services.

Finally, in 2005, I turned to self-employment to start 'Plus One Garden Services' to help local people with their gardens and properties. I referred to this new venture as *'Plus One'* because I knew that apart from Jesus I could do nothing. Jesus is my *'Plus One'* – He helps me in all that I do.

On a more personal level, Janet and I went to school together and then met again four years later in Guildford, Surrey, and immediately fell in love! Married in 1966, we have had three children. Lloyd, our firstborn, lived for only two months before he went to be with the Lord. Lloyd was followed by Deborah and then came Elizabeth. We now have five grandchildren – Anna, Sam, Amy, Hannah and Isaac.

So what about the question: "When was Jesus REALLY born?" – which was not on Christmas day! Janet and I have not observed Christmas in the traditional sense for about twenty years, from the time that we became aware that Christmas was not the correct time for Jesus' birth. In more recent years, I became curious to know why the Bible or ancient history did not state when Jesus was born. Why would such an important event not have been recorded? If the Bible was so clear about when Jesus died – at the time of the Jewish festival of Passover – then why did the Bible not give any indication of when Jesus was born? For me, it was a conundrum, a puzzle that needed to be solved.

After much prayer, study and thought, I began to identify a number of signs in Scripture which indicated that Jesus was born on the Jewish Day of Atonement. All the signs were recorded before Jesus was born, which is what I would have expected, knowing that when Jesus died was also recorded before His death.

For the four years or so that I've been occupied with these thoughts, my life has become a journey of insight and opportunity. My first attempt at publishing was to have printed a small booklet which gave details of the first two signs for the timing of Jesus' birth. Next came my book: *'He Must Increase…'* in which I included four signs, plus other insights into the life of Jesus. At the time of writing, I still have a few copies available. This, my latest book, *'When Was Jesus REALLY Born?'* brings things up-to-date with *Five Signs* and is why WhenWasJesusBorn.net has been launched.

Having read my first and second attempt at publishing, many have written to say that they do understand why Jesus was most likely to have been born on the Jewish Day of Atonement. Their response has been quite phenomenal and I'm so grateful to God for leading me to write what I have written. Therefore, I pray that you, too, will come to appreciate why God chose this particular day to be celebrated as a most *Awesome Day* – the day when Jesus was REALLY born?

Please note, however, the Day of Atonement is not a day for feasting and extravagance. Traditionally, for Jewish people, it is a day for prayer and fasting. Is this perhaps a more appropriate way for us to remember Jesus' birth, knowing what it must have meant to God to send to us His Son and what would eventually happen to Him on "An altar of earth…" (Exodus 20;24) outside of Jerusalem? I believe so, because He came and He died for me, and for you. And now He is risen. Praise God.

God Bless,

David Hamshire

ABOUT THE PUBLISHER

WRITE your book.
BUILD your brand.
CREATE your platform.
BROADCAST your message.
EXPAND your reach and income...

Perissos Media helps business owners, speakers, consultants, professionals, sales teams, ministry leaders and inspired individuals to PUBLISH books, audio and video products, in order to BUILD your platform and ELEVATE you to Expert Status in your field—with all the financial and lifestyle benefits that come with it.

What is your passion? Are you ready to go from LOCAL to GLOBAL?

Even if you have never written a word, we have resources and services to help you get your message out, one step at a time.

For a **<u>FREE GIFT</u>** to help you in building or expanding your platform, and to publish your message to a greater audience, please visit:

www.IWantToPublish.com

It has been our great pleasure to support David in the publication and promotion of this book. We look forward to serving you,

Jerry Kuzma
Director, PerissosMedia.com

FINAL REMARKS

If you have been helped by what I have written, may I suggest you share something about what you have learnt with another? Perhaps you could lend them this book? I know I cannot reach everyone, but <u>you</u> can help me to reach people I cannot reach, to help them understand Jesus.

If you would like to share a downloadable sample from this book, you can direct your friends and family to **WhenWasJesusBorn.net/sample.** Please share this link on Facebook, Twitter, and other social media sites as well.

If you disagree with something I have written, please contact me via the website and I will be happy to learn of your concerns.

My prayer in putting this book together is that its contents will have assisted you in considering Jesus as God's only Son:

> "…who for the joy that was set before Him
> endured the cross, despising the shame,
> and has sat down at the right hand
> of the throne of God." Hebrews 12:2

Send all comments to:

WhenWasJesusBorn.net/contact

4205691R00094

Printed in Germany
by Amazon Distribution
GmbH, Leipzig